C000041690

So you **really** want to learn

History
Britain 1485-1750
Answer Book

David Sharp

Series Editor: Niall Murphy M.A. (Cantab)

GALORE PARK

www.galorepark.co.uk

Published by Galore Park Publishing Ltd
19/21 Sayers Lane, Tenterden, Kent TN30 6BW

www.galorepark.co.uk

Text copyright © David Sharp 2009

The right of David Sharp to be identified as the author of this Work has been asserted by him in accordance with sections 77 and 78 of the Copyright, Designs and Patents Act 1988.

Typography by Typetechnique, London
Cover illustration by Ian Douglass

Printed and bound by CPI Antony Rowe, Chippenham

ISBN-13: 978 1 905735 07 5

All rights reserved: no part of this publication may be reproduced, stored in a retrieval system, or transmitted in any form or by any means, electronic, mechanical, photocopying, recording or otherwise, without either the prior written permission of the copyright owner or a licence permitting restricted copying issued by the Copyright Licensing Agency, 90 Tottenham Court Road, London W1P 0LP.

First published 2009

Details of other Galore Park publications are available at www.galorepark.co.uk

ISEB Revision Guides, publications and examination papers may also be obtained from Galore Park.

Contents

Introduction

The suggested answers in this book are designed to be informative rather than prescriptive and should be used as a guide on what to look for in and how to assess an answer. Each question is accompanied by a mark, all of which follow the Common Entrance mark scheme for history. The appendix at the back contains a copy of the mark scheme, which should help with the allocation of marks for a particular question.

Chapter 1 Henry VII, 1485–1509

Exercise 1.1

1. *Henry's claim to the throne was not a strong one. Although his mother, Lady Margaret Beaufort, was descended from Edward III, an Act of Parliament had made the Beauforts illegitimate, which meant that they could not claim the throne. However, Henry did have a claim if the Act of Parliament was ignored. In addition, he was far more popular than Richard III. (4 marks)*

2. (a) *The reason why Henry VII dated his reign from the day before the Battle of Bosworth was to show that his claim was not just based on his victory over Richard III. (2 marks)*
    (b) *The reason why Henry VII married Elizabeth of York was to unite the Houses of York and Lancaster and bring the Wars of the Roses to an end. (2 marks)*
    (c) *The reason why Henry VII called his son Arthur was because Arthur was the great legendary saviour king of England, so Henry wanted to associate his line with him. (2 marks)*

3. The description of Henry VII's problems and how he dealt with these should cover the following points:

    (a) *Henry VII's early problems as king included the following:*
    - *There were nobles who had become 'over-mighty subjects', i.e. noblemen who could challenge his authority and threaten his position as king.*
    - *The nobles had previously been allowed to keep their own private armies.*
    - *Some of these senior nobles had strong political power.*
    - *There were still some powerful high profile Yorkists who had fought against the King.*
    - *The priest Richard Symonds tried to pass off one of his pupils, Lambert Simnel, as Richard III's nephew Edward, who was rumoured to have been murdered.*
    - *Lambert Simnel received support from the Earl of Lincoln, who led a rebellion against the King. (20 marks)*

    (b) *Henry dealt with these problems as follows:*
    - *He dealt with the practice of retaining by restricting the size of the force a nobleman could keep.*
    - *He introduced recognisances – money held by the king that belonged to nobles, which could be forfeit if they misbehaved.*
    - *He used new middle class men as administrators on his council and as Justices of the Peace, so that the nobles had less influence.*

- *He reorganised and changed the use of the Court of Star Chamber, and re-established the Council of the North and the Council of Wales.*
- *He was able to defeat the Simnel rebellion and gained support of the Yorkists by having Elizabeth of York crowned queen.* (10 marks)

Total for exercise: 40 marks

Exercise 1.2

1. (a) The answer should contain the points highlighted below. A good answer should also include quotes from the *Registrum Annalium Collegii Mertonensis* as given on page 14.
    - *In 1489, the people of Yorkshire refused to pay a tax that was intended to pay for a war against France.*
    - *When the Earl of Northumberland tried to collect the money, he was attacked by a mob and killed.*
    - *The rebels were defeated.*
    - *In 1497, there was a rebellion in Cornwall due to tax.*
    - *Lord Audley collected together 15,000 men.*
    - *Perkin Warbeck joined the rebellion.*
    - *The rebels were defeated at Blackheath.* (20 marks)

    (b) The answer should include the following:
    - *Both the revolts were about taxation.*
    - *The Yorkshire rebellion was fairly minor. However, the Cornish rebellion was very serious.*
    - *Henry had to deal with the Cornish rebels personally.*
    - *The pretender Perkin Warbeck was involved in the Cornish rebellion.* (10 marks)

2. (a) The answer should contain the following points, including the dates of when the events occurred:
    - *Perkin Warbeck claimed to be Richard of York, the younger of the 'Princes in the Tower'.*
    - *He travelled to Ireland (1491), France and then to Burgundy (1492) to drum up support.*
    - *He was recognised as Richard by the Holy Roman Emperor (1493).*
    - *He had support from Scotland (1495).*
    - *He married the cousin of James IV (1496).*
    - *He led a Scots invasion into England but this failed (1496).*

- He joined the Cornish rebellion and was captured (1497).
- He escaped and was recaptured (1498), and then executed (1499). (20 marks)

(b) The explanation should contain the following points:
- Perkin Warbeck seemed to some to be a plausible claimant to the throne.
- He had some powerful support, i.e. Emperor Maximilian and James IV, King of Scotland.
- He had links with William Stanley, who had been so vital in Henry's victory at Bosworth and was a very powerful nobleman. (10 marks)

3. A good answer will include a discussion of whether or not Henry was a popular king. It should include the following material:
- Henry had to deal with the danger posed by a number of rebellions: the rebellion led by the Earl of Lincoln in support of Lambert Simnel; the large force involved in the Cornish rebellion; the involvement of William Stanley with Perkin Warbeck.
- Some of his taxes were unpopular which led to some of these rebellions.
- There was a constant general threat of noblemen who were too powerful, even though he put various systems in place to try and reduce their power.
- He came to the throne against a background of instability which had been inherited from the Wars of the Roses. (20 marks)

Total for exercise: 80 marks

Exercise 1.3

1. (a) Retaining was the practice of nobles keeping their own private armies. This meant that these nobles could be a threat to Henry. Henry restricted this practice to reduce the threat. (2 marks)

(b) Recognisances were a way of controlling the nobility by holding on to large sums of their money. The nobles would lose this money if they were not loyal to Henry and rebelled against him. (2 marks)

(c) Henry changed the Council so that only those nobles who were invited were allowed to attend. It became more efficient and professional, with specific people and committees responsible for specific tasks. (2 marks)

(d) Henry used the professional classes as officials in the Council and to advise him. These men included Richard Empson, Edmund Dudley, Reginald Bray and Edward Poynings. (2 marks)

(e) Henry used taxes to fund his war against France. These taxes led to the Yorkshire rebellion and the Cornish rebellion. (2 marks)

2. The answer should include all the different methods that Henry used. A good answer could include a quote from Polydore Vergils's assessment of him: 'Henry wished to keep all Englishmen obedient through fear ... when his subjects who were men of substance were found guilty of whatever fault he harshly fined them by a penalty which deprived them of their fortunes'.

Henry tried to control his nobility through a number of methods:
- *He introduced recognisances, whereby the nobles had to pay a large sum of money which they would lose if they were not loyal to the King.*
- *He distributed lands to lesser nobles and took land away from disloyal nobles.*
- *He changed the format of the Council so that you had to be invited to attend, and used the professional classes rather than nobles to advise him and run the Council.*
- *He increased the power of the Court of Star Chamber to deal with rebellions and appointed Justices of the Peace from the gentry and professional classes rather than nobles.*
- *He re-established the Council of the North and the Council of Wales so that he did not have to rely on the nobles in these areas.* (20 marks)

3. (a) *Henry's foreign policy included the following:*
- *In 1489, he signed the Treaty of Medina del Campo with Spain. In this treaty he agreed that his son Arthur would marry Catherine of Aragon, the daughter of King Ferdinand and Queen Isabella of Spain.*
- *In 1492, he signed the treaty of Etaples with France.*
- *In 1502, he agreed to the marriage of his daughter Margaret to James IV of Scotland.*
- *In 1508, he betrothed his other daughter Mary to the Archduke Charles of Burgundy, although this marriage never took place.* (20 marks)

(b) *Henry's main aim in foreign policy was to make his throne secure and to prevent other monarchs giving assistance to pretenders who wished to overthrow him:*
- *The Treaty of Medina del Campo showed that he was a powerful, legitimate monarch because the Spanish sovereigns were prepared to marry their daughter to his son.*
- *The Treaty of Etaples got the King of France on his side after the Perkin Warbeck affair. Warbeck had had assistance from France.*
- *The marriage of his daughter to James IV of Scotland stopped any claimants to the throne using Scotland as a base to invade England.* (10 marks)

4.

Henry VII's reign	
Successes	**Failures**
Made England peaceful after the Wars of the Roses	Was never popular and many hated him
Curbed the nobility	Seen as a miser and a tyrant
Put down rebellion	Never felt the Tudor dynasty was secure
Made the crown more powerful and rich	Introduced taxes which led to rebellion

(10 marks)

(a) *Henry established himself as King by:*
- *Defeating Richard III.*
- *Marrying Elizabeth of York, thus uniting the two warring houses of York and Lancaster.*
- *Curbing the nobility by re-distributing land, introducing recognisances, changing the functioning of the Council and the Court of Star Chamber, and re-establishing the Council of the North and the Council of Wales.*
- *Defeating the two pretenders Lambert Simnel and Perkin Warbeck.* (20 marks)

(b) *Overall Henry VII was successful as a king for the following reasons:*
- *He inherited a country torn apart by the Wars of the Roses and he provided strong, stable government.*
- *The Crown had been weak, partly because it was poor. Henry made it quite rich.*
- *He dealt with the problem of potentially dangerous 'over-mighty subjects', the aristocracy, by curbing their powers. He was so secure he could even execute a former ally, Stanley, when he allied himself with Warbeck.*
- *He defeated both pretenders: at the Battle of East Stoke he defeated the Earl of Lincoln and Simnel in 1487, and dealt with the next challenge Warbeck, executing him together with the Earl of Warwick. Henceforth he was secure on the throne.*
- *He was never loved, but he was feared and, despite his own worries about the security of the Tudor dynasty, his son Henry VIII succeeded him without opposition.* (10 marks)

Total for exercise: 100 marks

Chapter 2 Henry VIII, 1509–1547

Exercise 2.1

1. The answer to this question will be subjective but the following might well be noticed:
    - Slimness
    - Sensitivity
    - Youth
    - Intelligence (5 marks)

2. The answer to this question will again be subjective (to a lesser extent) but the answer could contain references to:
    - Wealth
    - Power
    - Virility
    - Arrogance (5 marks)

3. A good answer should include a physical description as well as quotes from Lord Mountjoy, John Taylor, Sagudino and Giustiniani:
    - *The young Henry VIII was a tall, slim man who was both handsome and athletic.*
    - *He was intelligent, speaking Latin, French, Italian and Spanish, as well as being good at mathematics and theology.*
    - *He is described by Giustiniani as 'athletic and highly intelligent'.*
    - *He excelled at sport. When practising archery, he is described by John Taylor as having 'surpassed them all'.*
    - *He had boundless energy, being able to joust for three hours, where he 'excelled all others'.* (10 marks)
    - *The 1509 portrait shows the King as young, immature and sensitive; while the 1537 portrait shows a mature, powerful monarch.*
    - *Both portraits show jewellery and fine clothing, denoting wealth and rank.* (5 marks)

4. A good answer should include quotes from some of the sources of Lord Mountjoy, John Taylor, Sagudino and Giustiniani:
    - *The term 'Renaissance prince' implies wide learning in a variety of subjects, as well as music and perhaps even physical prowess.*
    - *Renaissance prince is a good term to describe Henry VIII because he had a wide-ranging education.*

- Giustiniani says of him: 'He speaks good French, Latin and Spanish ... He devotes himself to pleasure'.
- He wrote poetry and several pieces of music.
- He was interested in architecture and was involved in the construction and improvement of several prominent buildings. (20 marks)

5. Hans Holbein's career should include the following points:
- Hans Holbein was born in 1497 in Augsburg, Germany.
- He was a German artist, called the 'Younger' to distinguish him from his painter father, Hans.
- He worked for a while in Basel, then found international fame with a portrait of Erasmus, who introduced him to the humanist circle of Sir Thomas More.
- He then worked for Anne Boleyn and Thomas Cromwell.
- He was appointed painter to Henry VIII.
- His portraits of the members of Henry's court are a unique record of a court, but his most famous painting is 'The Ambassadors', a double portrait of the French ambassador and a visiting French bishop.
- He painted Anne of Cleves before Henry VIII saw her.
- He died in 1543. (20 marks)

Erasmus's career should include the following points:
- Erasmus was born in 1466 in the Netherlands.
- He was a theologian and scholar.
- He was critical of some aspects of the Catholic Church and especially the corruption of the Pope.
- He published Julius Exclusis, an attack on Pope Julius II whom Erasmus saw as being excluded from heaven because of his corruption.
- He moved around European universities, giving lectures which made him famous.
- He published popular satires and editions of the scriptures.
- He was a friend of Sir Thomas More and other English humanists.
- He was the most famous and influential scholar of his time.
- He died in 1536. (20 marks)

Total for exercise: 85 marks

Exercise 2.2

1. (a) *Indulgences were payments made to the Church for reducing time in Purgatory.*
        (2 marks)

    (b) *Fidei Defensor was the title given to Henry by the Pope for writing against Luther.*
        (2 marks)

    (c) *Purgatory is 'The place of waiting', where the soul is purged of all its sins.*
        After Purgatory the soul can go to Heaven or Hell. (2 marks)

2. (a) A good answer should contain comments on corruption, wealth and the role
        of priests, including the following:
        - *Pluralism began to cause resentment. This was where bishops and priests held
          more than one office, paying someone else to carry out their duties but taking
          most of the income themselves. Thomas Wolsey was one of these priests.*
        - *The Church controlled vast amounts of land.*
        - *The Church was failing to look after the poor and fulfil its charitable obligations.*
        - *Services were incomprehensible for most people as they were in Latin.*
        - *There was no English bible.*
        - *Martin Luther, a German monk, made a list of ninety-five criticisms, the main
          one being the buying of indulgences to reduce time in Purgatory. These ideas
          spread. (20 marks)*

    (b) A good answer should show a connection between all the points in (a) and
        the growing dissatisfaction with the church:
        - *The resentment that had grown due to pluralism, the fact that the Church
          controlled vast amounts of land and was failing to look after the poor, created a
          climate where Henry could break from Rome.*
        - *This led to the Reformation Parliament, which reflected public disquiet with the
          Church, and led to the cutting back of the power and influence of the Pope.*
        - *With the birth of Protestantism, following the spread of Martin Luther's
          criticism, there were changing attitudes to the Roman Catholic Church and its
          powers. (10 marks)*

3. (a) The answer should show Wolsey in a negative way:
        - *Wolsey was seen as corrupt, greedy, self-seeking and ambitious.*
        - *He was disliked because he was seen as a 'humble' churchman in a too
          powerful position with influence over the King.*
        - *He was involved in pluralism, which was resented by many ordinary people.*
        - *He failed to secure Henry an annulment for his marriage to Catherine of
          Aragon.*

- *Cranmer was influenced by Protestant ideas.*
- *He was prepared to defy the Pope and legalise the annulment of Henry's marriage to Catherine of Aragon.*
- *He married Henry to Anne Boleyn. (20 marks)*

(b) Pupils could argue the case for either man playing the most significant part. Some of the following points could be included:

- *Wolsey's part in the events of the period were largely negative – his failings and failure to obtain the annulment pushed Henry towards the break from Rome.*
- *Cranmer became Henry's obedient servant and gave religious sanction to both the annulment and the marriage, which many people accepted.*
- *Therefore, this could indicate that Cranmer played the more significant role in the long term. (10 marks)*

4. (a) *The religious views held by Henry VIII at the time of the break from Rome were as follows:*

- *Henry was a conservative Roman Catholic.*
- *He was not a Protestant and had written a book attacking Martin Luther and defending the Roman Catholic Church.*
- *He was awarded the title Fidei Defensor (Defender of the Faith) by the Pope.*
- *However, the Pope would not agree to the annulment of his marriage to Catherine of Aragon.*
- *On hearing of Henry's marriage to Anne Boleyn, which was carried out by the new Archbishop of Canterbury, Thomas Cranmer, the Pope excommunicated Henry.*
- *However, Henry had begun to believe that the Pope had no authority in England, and therefore his excommunication did not matter.*
- *Therefore, Henry believed he could be Head of the Church in England rather than the Pope. (20 marks)*

(b) *Henry's views affected the way in which he became Head of the Church of England in the following ways:*

- *The religious views held in answer (a) meant that Henry did not want a break from Rome in order to create a Protestant church.*
- *He began to believe that his marriage to Catherine of Aragon was not legal in the eyes of God and the Church. This was why he had not been blessed with a son – God was punishing him for his sin in marrying his brother's widow: 'If a man shall take his brother's wife it is an unclean thing … they shall be childless' Leviticus 20:21. Without a son, the dynasty would fail.*

- He fell deeply in love with Anne Boleyn, as can be seen from some of the letters he wrote to her: '... having been for a whole year struck with the dart of love'; '... but that I would you were in my arms or I in yours for I think it long since I kissed you'.
- He became convinced that Anne would give him the son he craved.
- By becoming Head of the Church in England he could control it, make its laws and therefore secure the annulment of his marriage to Catherine of Aragon. (10 marks)

5. (a) The main Acts of the Reformation Parliament were:
   - The Act in Restraint of Annates of 1532, which stopped all payments to the Pope from the English Church.
   - The Statute in Restraint of Appeals of 1533, which forbade appeals to Rome, stating that England was an empire governed by one supreme head and king who possessed 'whole and entire' authority within the realm, and that no judgements or excommunications from Rome were valid. It prevented Catherine of Aragon appealing to the Pope.
   - The Act of Succession of 1533, which declared the marriage to Catherine of Aragon to have been unlawful, rendering Princess Mary illegitimate. It stated that the heirs to the throne would be the children of Henry and Anne Boleyn.
   - The Act of Supremacy of 1534, which made Henry the Head of the English Church instead of the Pope.
   - The Treason Act of 1534, which meant that anyone who denied Henry's position as Head of the Church could be tried for treason.
   - The First Fruits and Tenths Act of 1534, which permitted Henry to take the first year's revenue from all bishoprics and benefices. All clerics then had to pay one tenth of their income to the Crown. (20 marks)

   (b) These were significant in the way Henry achieved control over the Church of England for the following reasons:
   - The 1532 Act in Restraint of Annates was designed to (i) channel revenues from Rome to the Crown; and (ii) make it clear to the Pope that Henry had the power to control the Church in England.
   - The 1533 Statute in Restraint of Appeals (i) pointed at Henry's power over the Church in England and, in theory, declared it independent from the power of the Pope; and (ii), on a practical level, stopped appeals by Catherine of Aragon to Rome, so she had no further hope that the Pope could help her prevent the divorce from Henry.

- *The 1533 Act of Succession (i) declared the marriage to Catherine of Aragon unlawful, which meant that Henry's daughter by that marriage, Princess Mary, was illegitimate and had no claim to the throne; and (ii), as Henry was convinced that Anne Boleyn would produce a male child, that child would be Henry's rightful heir under the Act.*
- *The 1534 Act of Supremacy laid down by Act of Parliament that the Pope's authority was finally and absolutely rejected and the rightful head of the Church was the monarch.*
- *The 1534 Treason Act was designed to prevent people objecting to Henry's claim to be head of the Church. It was now treason to say or write that he was not.*
- *The 1534 First Fruits and Tenths Act laid down that the Church had to pay ten per cent income tax to the Crown, and that the considerable income of bishops went to the Crown in their first year in office.*

The most important Act was the Act of Supremacy:
- *It made clear what the previous Acts were moving towards, i.e. the break from Rome.*
- *It stabilised the authority of the Crown over the Church.*
- *It created the Church of England, which survives to this day.*
- *By the Act of Supremacy, the monarch could make laws to govern the Church, so Henry could do what he wanted without reference to the Pope. (10 marks)*

Total for exercise: 126 marks

Exercise 2.3

1. *The marriage was to cement the alliance between England and Spain. Arthur and Catherine had been childless, so it is implied that if Henry and Catherine have a child this will further unite the two countries. (2 marks)*

2. *They agree that Henry had fallen in love with Anne Boleyn; 'shall be yours' implies divorce from Catherine. Haigh suggests love for Anne and divorce from Catherine went together, and that is implied in Source B. (3 marks)*

3. In this type of question quotations from and intelligent use of the sources to give a balanced coherent answer is important, whatever the conclusion reached.
   A possible answer is as follows:
   - *Source B is a contemporary source, whereas Source C is written by a modern historian.*

- *Haigh is able to balance all the evidence and be, perhaps, impartial so this source is more balanced.*
- *However, Henry's letter to Anne gives us an insight into how he felt at the time and therefore can be seen to be more valuable.* (7 marks)

4. The following points should be included in the answer:
    - *Source A shows that politics was the most important factor in Henry's marriage to Catherine of Aragon, rather than love.*
    - *Source B shows that Henry appears to have fallen deeply in love with Anne Boleyn.*
    - *Source C gives a balance between love for Anne and desire for a male heir.*
    - *Given that Henry's marriage to Catherine had a strong political motivation, and as part of Henry's desire to marry Anne was in order to produce the desired heir, then, on balance, the King's 'great matter' was one of politics (the succession) rather than love, although love undoubtedly played a part.* (8 marks)

Total for exercise: 20 marks

Exercise 2.4

1. (a) *Baptism is the sprinkling of water by a priest as a blessing on a child in order to initiate the child into the church.* (2 marks)

    (b) *Penance is the praying for forgiveness of sins; in order to have these sins forgiven one had to truly repent.* (2 marks)

    (c) *The eucharist celebrated the Last Supper by the consecration of bread and wine.* (2 marks)

    (d) *The Six Articles were a move back to conservative religious observances and beliefs, as Henry became worried about the spread of Protestantism. They stated a Catholic position on transubstantiation, clerical celibacy, confession and taking of communion. The Articles were disliked by Protestants.* (2 marks)

    (e) *The King's Book tried to prevent the lower orders from reading the Bible in English. The hope was that this would prevent them having their own ideas about religion by reading the Bible, as Bible reading was very important to the spread of Protestant ideas.* (2 marks)

2. (a) The answer should contain the following points:
    - *There was a possibility of war with both Francis I of France and Charles V King of Spain, the Holy Roman Emperor, because of Henry's break from Rome. Therefore, Henry needed money to fund these wars and the monasteries were rich.*

- *Thomas Cromwell was given the title of Vicar General in 1535. This gave him power over the Church.*
- *Cromwell initiated the Valor Ecclasiasticus to find out the exact wealth of religious houses. He sent commissioners to discover if the monasteries were corrupt (the visitations).*
- *The visitations made a case against the monasteries, but often reports were exaggerated or biased.*
- *To some Protestants, the monasteries were seen as places of huge wealth which allowed monks to live in drunken debauchery.*
- *The monasteries were also seen by some as providing a vast source of income for the Pope in Rome.*
- *In 1536 smaller houses (those with an income of under £200 a year) were dissolved; in 1539 larger houses were also dissolved. (20 marks)*

(b) *Henry and Cromwell had different reasons for dissolving the monasteries:*
- *Henry's reason for dissolving the monasteries was not due to possible corruption but because they were wealthy and he needed the money to strengthen the Crown and to build defences and fund possible wars with France and Spain.*
- *Cromwell's reasons were probably more complicated. He did want to make Henry richer, but as he was a Protestant sympathiser, he saw the monasteries as centres of possible Roman Catholic resistance to religious change, as well as being superstitious.*
- *Henry and Cromwell were totally successful in dissolving the religious houses partly because local landowners were pleased to get a share of the spoils. (10 marks)*

3. (a) A good answer should use evidence from page 37 from the oath of the rebels and Hall's chronicle.

   The aims of Aske and Darcy in the Pilgrimage of Grace were as follows:
   - *Aske and Darcy were religious conservatives and they wished to reverse the religious changes.*
   - *They wished to remove heretics such as Cromwell and Cranmer from the King's council.*
   - *They wanted Mary to be seen as Henry's legitimate daughter.*
   - *They wished to halt enclosure, stop abuses by corrupt officials and reform Parliamentary elections.*
   - *They also demanded the repeal of the harsh Treason Act. (20 marks)*

(b) The answer should contain the following points:
- *Although the rebels were eventually defeated, Henry did move in a more conservative direction with the Six Articles.*
- *The monasteries, supported by the pilgrims, were, however, dissolved.*
- *They therefore failed in achieving their aims.* (**10 marks**)

4. (a) Pupils will need to consult the map on page 37 in order to answer this question.

The main events of the Pilgrimage of Grace were as follows:
- *In 1536 a revolt broke out in Lincolnshire when the commissioners came to close the monasteries there.*
- *This rebellion was quickly put down by the Duke of Suffolk.*
- *The unrest then moved to Yorkshire, when Robert Aske and Lord Darcy raised 30,000 men.*
- *By the October the rebels had moved south.*
- *The Duke of Norfolk was sent to intercept the pilgrims at Doncaster. Norfolk, however, did not have enough troops to fight the rebels, so instead he offered them pardons and promised them a Parliament to deal with their demands.*
- *The rebels then dispersed.*
- *When another revolt broke out in the north-west in January 1537, it gave Henry the excuse to arrest and execute Aske and 170 other rebel ringleaders.* (**20 marks**)

(b) A good answer should include the following points:
- *Henry regarded the pilgrims as rebels because their demands included putting Mary back in the line of succession and an end to the attacks on the monasteries, which Henry had already decided on.*
- *The revolt at first showed Henry's weakness as he did not have enough troops to fight the rebels.*
- *Eventually, however, it showed his strength as he was able to disperse the rebels because they trusted his word as King.* (**10 marks**)

Total for exercise: **100 marks**

Exercise 2.5

1. Information about each of the wives should include the following:
    *   Catherine of Aragon. (a) The reason for the marriage was to cement an alliance with Spain. (b) There was one daughter, Mary. (c) The marriage was annulled. Catherine died in 1536. (3 marks)
    *   Anne Boleyn. (a) The reason for the marriage was that Henry fell in love with her and was convinced she would provide a male heir. (b) There was one daughter, Elizabeth. (c) Anne was executed for adultery in May 1536, although the evidence was framed. (3 marks)
    *   Jane Seymour. (a) Henry seems, again, to have married for love. (b) There was one son, Edward. (c) Jane died from complications in childbirth. (3 marks)
    *   Anne of Cleves. (a) The marriage was for diplomatic reasons in order to create a Protestant alliance, urged by Cromwell. (b) There were no children. (c) Henry found her unattractive and so divorced her. The failure of the Cleves marriage led to Cromwell's downfall. (3 marks)
    *   Catherine Howard. (a) Henry again fell in love. (b) There were no children. (c) Catherine was executed for adultery, but this time the evidence was probably not false. (3 marks)
    *   Catherine Parr. (a) The reasons for this marriage were probably that she was quiet and so appealed to Henry in his increasingly ill state. (b) There were no children. (c) Catherine survived Henry and remarried. (3 marks)

2. This is an exercise in using historical imagination and should be seen in that context. Credit can be given for use of sources and research. (15 marks)

Total for exercise: 33 marks

Exercise 2.6

1. Source A shows the following about Henry VIII:
    *   Henry had personal charm.
    *   He used this to win over people.
    *   Underneath he was selfish and ruthless.
    *   Friendship really meant little to him. (2 marks)

2. Source B agrees with Source A as it shows Henry being charming and friendly:
    *   Source B shows Henry trying to use charm, 'love and favour you'.
    *   He appears to be appealing for harmony. (3 marks)

3. *Source C shows that friendship with Henry VIII influenced the subjects' lifestyle in the following ways:*
   - *Henry rewarded his closest advisors.*
   - *They could live a very rich lifestyle.*

   In the answer reference could be made to Hampton Court as Wolsey's palace. (7 marks)

4. A good answer to this question will use all the sources and give a balanced assessment. A possible answer could argue that winning affection and getting his own way were part of his style of kingship and cannot be easily separated.

   References to his charm and ruthlessness should be included to support the answer. (8 marks)

   Total for exercise: 20 marks

Chapter 3 Edward VI and Mary I

Exercise 3.1

1. The following points should be included for the Dukes of Somerset and Northumberland:
   - *The Duke of Somerset was Edward Seymour 1505–1552.*
   - *He was a courtier to Henry VIII and soldier.*
   - *He was appointed Lord Protector on the death of Henry VIII.*
   - *He was a Protestant and abolished chantries.*
   - *After two rebellions in 1549, the Western Rising and Kett's Rebellion, he was seen as weak and deposed by his rival Northumberland.*
   - *Because of his leniency and cancelling of the treason laws he was known as the 'good Duke'.*
   - *He was executed in January 1552.*

   - *The Duke of Northumberland was John Dudley, Earl of Warwick 1504–1554.*
   - *He was a statesman and soldier.*
   - *He led an attack on Boulogne in 1544, defeated the Scots at Pinkie in 1547 and put down the Kett's rebellion.*
   - *He was seen as ruthless and self-seeking.*
   - *After ousting Somerset he became chief minister and controlled Edward but did not make himself Protector.*
   - *He was an even stronger Protestant than Somerset, but was probably only really interested in getting his hands on bishops' lands when he had conservative bishops replaced by strong Protestants.*
   - *He was executed in 1554 after the failure of the Lady Jane Grey plot of 1553.*
   (10 marks)

2. The following points should be included for John Calvin:
   - *John Calvin was a stricter Protestant than Luther.*
   - *He set up a Protestant state in Geneva and his writings were sent all over Europe from there.*
   - *He believed in predestination – the idea that if God knew everything, then God would know who would go to heaven (the saved) before they were even born.*
   - *Calvinism was associated with the smashing of images in churches (iconoclasm) and strict moral codes.* (5 marks)

3. The following points should be included for the Act of Uniformity of 1549:
    - *The most important aspect of the Act was the use of English in all church services.*
    - *The Act introduced communion using both bread and wine.*
    - *It showed the way Cranmer's Protestant ideas were developing.*
    - *It made all church services conform by composing the first Book of Common Prayer.* (5 marks)

4. The following points should be included for the Prayer Books:
    - *The Prayer Book of 1549 was composed by Cranmer.*
    - *It was written in English rather than Latin.*
    - *It was Protestant in its forms but was rather vague on the issue of transubstantiation.*
    - *The Prayer Book of 1552 was known as the Book of Common Prayer.*
    - *Transubstantiation was denied and communion was made commemorative.*
    - *There were some changes to some terms, e.g. Lord's table was substituted for altar; the eucharist was named the Lord's Supper.*
    - *It made moves towards a strong Calvinist Protestant position.* (5 marks)

Total for exercise: 25 marks

Exercise 3.2

1. *The picture is trying to show:*
    - *Henry passing his throne to his son Edward.*
    - *A united council supporting Edward.*
    - *The overthrow of the Pope, who is shown as being crushed down and defeated.*
    - *The destruction of what the Protestants saw as superstitious images of Roman Catholicism.* (2 marks)

2. Note that the answer needs to show understanding that 'suffer' means to allow something as well as finding something painful.
    - *Source B shows that Protestantism was the official faith and the true one as far as Edward was concerned.*
    - *Even Mary was pressurised to convert to Protestantism.*
    - *Mary was not prepared to change her religion, or to pretend to do so.* (3 marks)

3. *Source C tells us the following about Edward's religious teaching:*
    - *This is a letter from Calvin to Edward VI offering advice and support for the policies of Northumberland and Cranmer.*

- *It gives a thorough insight into Protestant views on prayers for the dead, frivolities, saints, including 'purity', meaning the taking away of all Catholic ceremonies and ideas.*
- *It is implied that Edward has been properly instructed in religion and that God will support him as a Protestant prince. (7 marks)*

4. A good answer should include the following points:
   - *Source A is propaganda for the Protestant church and shows how Edward and his advisors on the council have pulled down 'false' Roman Catholic practices and defeated the Pope. It is, of course, biased.*
   - *Source B shows that Catholicism has survived with a potentially strong supporter, Mary, who is next in line to the throne. Given that Edward was a strong Protestant and that he disapproved of Mary's religion, then it is almost certainly an accurate statement of Mary's position, as well as of his dislike of it.*
   - *Calvin's letter to Edward is designed to offer support and advice from his strong Protestant point of view. This is shown by his statement that 'God does not allow' various Catholic practices. Calvin is writing to the converted, so it supports the other two sources in showing the atmosphere of Protestant thinking that surrounded Edward VI. (8 marks)*

Total for exercise: 20 marks

Exercise 3.3

1. This is a brief extract where it is useful to look at the background to the Western Rebellion before answering the question.
   - *The Western Rebellion was a conservative rebellion. The rebels wished to have the Catholic practices and ceremonies reinstated, hence 'holy decrees of our forefathers'.*
   - *Those who did not agree with their conservative religious views were condemned as heretics, 'who so ever shall gainsay them, we hold as heretics'.*
   - *The Western Rebellion was partly against services in English, which many Cornish people did not speak. (5 marks)*

2. A good answer should include the following similarities and differences:
   - *There were the following similarities between the two rebellions:*
     - *The reason why both rebellions started was due to financial problems – in the case of the Western Rebellion this was due to taxes; in the case of the Kett's Rebellion, this was due to high land rents.*
     - *There was a capture of a major city in each case – Exeter and Norwich.*
     - *There was temporary loss of control by the government.*

- There were the following differences between the two rebellions:
  - Kett's rebels had no objection to the religious changes, in fact they used the new Prayer Book; whilst the Western rebels were religious conservatives/Catholics. (5 marks)

Total for exercise: 10 marks

Exercise 3.4

1. (a) A good answer should include the following points:
   - The source is contemporary.
   - Renard was a Catholic so was not sympathetic to Protestantism, yet he is forced to admit the problems that a return to Catholicism might have, therefore, this source can be regarded as reliable.
   - Phrases such as 'cruel' and 'bear pain' show that Renard can see the point of view of Protestants, although he does not agree with them. Therefore, this is a very useful piece of evidence, but it is confined to London. (5 marks)

   (b) The following points should be included in the answer:
   - This does support the cruelty suggested by Renard, and Foxe implies that Cranmer's execution was unpopular: 'amazement and indignation'.
   - However, there is not a great deal of evidence from Foxe about public reaction, as opposed to an emotional account of Cranmer's death. Therefore, this is not a particularly useful source compared with Renard with regard to public opinion. (5 marks)

2.

Deserves nickname	Does not deserve nickname
Defeated Wyatt rebellion and had 120 rebels hanged	Imprisoned Elizabeth in the Tower and then at Woodstock but did not have her executed
Wyatt was executed and his head stuck on a spike	Used training and supervision of parish priests to help them fulfil their duties
Had Lady Jane Grey and her husband Guildford Dudley executed	
Had Lady Jane Grey's father executed	
Imprisoned Cranmer in the Tower and then had him burned at the stake	
Heretics were burned at the stake	

Mary does deserve the name 'Bloody Mary' because she had many people burnt at the stake during her reign, the burnings becoming more frequent as Mary's reign progressed. (5 marks)

3. This is an exercise in using historical imagination and should be seen in that context. (10 marks)

Total for exercise: 25 marks

Exercise 3.5

1. *Source A tells us the following about Cranmer's death:*
   - *Source A is biased towards Protestantism, 'thus he died a martyr for truth', so the writer sees Protestantism as the true religion.*
   - *He takes the view that Cranmer was a hero who only recanted because of his ill treatment in prison, 'body weakened by confinement in prison and persistent persecution'.*
   - *However, despite his bias, his account of Cranmer's death tallies with other historical sources, including Foxe.*
   - *It shows Cranmer eventually becoming a Protestant and martyr, being prepared to put his hand into the flames because it 'hath offended' by signing the recantation. (2 marks)*

2. *Sources A and B agree in the following ways:*
   - *Both sources are by historians writing after the events, in both cases in the 20th century.*
   - *They agree about the way that Protestants were seen as martyrs for their faith: 'his humiliation was turned into a triumph', 'the Lord strengthen thee', 'a large crowd called the Lord strengthen them'.*
   - *So both sources agree on the way that the executions were seen by other Protestants as martyrdom. (3 marks)*

3. The answer in relation to Source C should include the following:
   - *Source C is from Foxe's Book of Martyrs and shows helpless, naked women and a child being burnt to death.*
   - *It is therefore a very emotional picture designed to show Protestants how much some of their fellow believers had suffered.*
   - *It is therefore useful to an historian because it shows the emotion and high feeling that the executions created. (7 marks)*

4. A good answer should cover the following points:
    - *All the sources tend to show that the executions of Protestants had actually made Protestantism more popular, as people reacted against what they saw as cruel persecution.*
    - *The burnings are depicted in every source as appallingly cruel.*
    - *The reaction of many is shown by the phrases 'large crowds', 'the Lord comfort them', 'out of his misery he rose'.*
    - *Foxe's Book of Martyrs was widely read after Mary's death and helped to advance the Protestant cause.* (8 marks)

                                                    Total for exercise: 20 marks

Exercise 3.6

1. A good answer should include the following points:
    - *Foxe is useful because, despite his anti-Catholicism, he shows the depth of feeling engendered by the burning of Protestants under Mary.*
    - *Despite his desire to put Catholicism in a poor light, Foxe is actually quite accurate about the details of the martyrs he writes about.*
    - *Therefore, he is a very useful source, even with his definite Protestant bias.* (5 marks)

2. The following points should be included in the answer:
    - *Protestantism seems to have spread more rapidly and put down more roots in London and the Home counties.*
    - *This may have been because literacy in London was greater, books were easily passed round there and the remoter parts of the country (the North and West) were always more conservative, as seen, for example, by the Pilgrimage of Grace and Western Rebellion.* (5 marks)

3. A good answer would include most of the following points:
    - *It was merchants from London in particular who were involved in importing Protestant books from abroad.*
    - *Merchants such as the grocer Richard Grafton, a rich London spice importer, actually paid for a translation of the Bible into English, as well as distributing other Protestant material.*
    - *Merchants tended to have more contact with Europe and the religious movements there.*
    - *Craftsmen were self-educated, could read and studied their English Bibles to make up their minds independently and tended to reject the Church's authority.*

- *The nobles, although they had benefited by the dissolution of the monasteries, tended to be more conservative and were more inclined to try to keep in favour with the monarch.*
- *Many of the nobility were, if not outright Roman Catholics, much more sympathetic to Catholicism than Protestantism, which some saw as looking to overturn the social order.*
- *They did not like merchants and craftsmen having their own, independent opinions.* (10 marks)

Total for exercise: 20 marks

Chapter 4 Elizabeth I, 1558–1603

Exercise 4.1

1. At the start of her reign, Elizabeth faced the following problems:
    *   The Crown was poor.
    *   She was faced with war with France – the French king claimed that Elizabeth was illegitimate.
    *   She had the very serious problem of religion. There had been a series of religious upheavals through the reigns of Henry VIII, Edward VI and Mary. Most people who were not deep thinkers or religious were simply confused, but Elizabeth had to find some kind of compromise between strongly held views by a minority of her subjects.
    *   Being a female monarch in the 16th century was itself a problem. Both Matilda and Mary, earlier female rulers, had not been seen by many as successful monarchs and the whole idea of rule by a woman was difficult to accept. (5 marks)

2. (a) Elizabeth found herself faced with religious problems caused by two extremes in religious thought and practice, Catholics and Puritans.
    *   Most Catholics were loyal to Elizabeth, although they did not agree with the Elizabethan Settlement of the Church of England. But some Catholics saw it as their duty to overthrow Elizabeth and return England to Roman Catholicism.
    *   The Pope excommunicated Elizabeth in 1570 and therefore, in theory, made all Catholics oppose her.
    *   The Northern Rebellion and the plots surrounding Mary Queen of Scots posed direct threats to Elizabeth.
    *   Catholic priests trained abroad kept the Catholic faith alive in England.
    *   Puritans were extreme Protestants who thought that Elizabeth's compromise religious settlement was not Protestant enough. They wished to push the Anglican Church in a Calvinist direction.
    *   There was an important group of Puritan MPs in the House of Commons, and with Puritan preachers and lecturers such as Cartwright, they wished to do away with bishops altogether.
    *   It is important to stress that in the sixteenth and seventeenth centuries Puritanism was not a coherent absolute set of beliefs; there were moderate and extreme Puritans, some were prepared to accept bishops, others were not. (20 marks)

(b) Elizabeth set about solving these issues in the following ways:
- Elizabeth was determined to defend the 1559 Settlement and the Thirty-Nine Articles against attacks from both Catholics and Puritans.
- Elizabeth tried to create a compromise that would satisfy as many people as possible. The amalgamation of the previous two Prayer Books (1549 and 1559) left the question of communion open to different interpretations, so that those of differing beliefs could still worship.
- Elizabeth did not call herself Supreme Head of the Church but Supreme Governor. Head and governor have slightly different meanings so that those who believed that the Pope should be the spiritual head of the Church might not be offended.
- Elizabeth appointed moderate bishops, not more extreme Puritans, and some bishops made efforts to get on with Puritans within their diocese. (10 marks)

3. (a) A good answer should include the following points:
- Roman Catholics opposed the Elizabethan Settlement because despite the Supreme Governor title (rather than Supreme Head), many believed that the Pope should be the only ruler of the Church.
- Some Catholic ideas such as transubstantiation, the cult of saints and the Virgin Mary were condemned by the Settlement.
- As the Pope had excommunicated Elizabeth, all Catholics should have opposed her.
- A minority of Catholics believed Mary Queen of Scots to be the rightful Queen.
- Puritans believed the Settlement was too much of a compromise with conservative/Catholic views.
- They believed that the Church should be purified of images, clerical vestments and bishops.
- They wanted a more radical Prayer Book. (20 marks)

(b) Elizabeth knew she needed to accommodate moderate Catholics and Protestants:
- Elizabeth had realised that different religious views were potentially dangerous. There had been so many rapid changes in the last thirty years that the country needed peace through compromise.
- She was reluctant to persecute people for their religious beliefs and hoped that she could unite all the differing views within a broad English compromise Settlement.
- She hoped this would prevent disorder, treason and rebellion. (10 marks)

Total for exercise: 65 marks

Exercise 4.2

1. The answer, either written or as a cartoon, should contain a clear understanding of Mary's family line, the Darnley marriage, the Rizzio murder, the birth of James, the Darnley murder and the Bothwell marriage. (5 marks)

2. (a) *There were several Catholic plots against Elizabeth:*
    *   *The Northern Rebellion*
        *   *– The Northern Rebellion involved the Catholic, Howard, Duke of Norfolk.*
        *   *– He planned to marry Mary.*
        *   *– When Elizabeth found out, the Duke of Norfolk was sent to the Tower of London, which led to rebellion in the North.*
        *   *– This was a real threat because of possible Spanish help.*
        *   *– The rebels were defeated and many executed.*
    *   *The Ridolfi Plot*
        *   *– This was again a plot to put Mary on the throne along with the Duke of Norfolk.*
        *   *– The plot was discovered by one of Sir Francis Walsingham's spies.*
        *   *– The Duke of Norfolk was executed.*
    *   *The Throckmorton Plot*
        *   *– Francis Throckmorton took letters written by Mary to the Spanish Ambassador and, by extension, to Philip II asking for help.*
        *   *– These were discovered by Sir Francis Walsingham's spies, although Walsingham may have used forged letters to incriminate Mary.*
        *   *– Throckmorton and other conspirators were executed but Elizabeth was still anxious not to punish Mary.*
    *   *The Babington Plot*
        *   *– Sir Francis Walsingham's spies intercepted letters from a Catholic, Anthony Babington, although, again, some have argued that Walsingham may have tampered with the evidence in order to incriminate Mary.*
        *   *– In effect, Mary called for the overthrow of Elizabeth by force; this was treason. Babington himself was to kill Elizabeth.*
        *   *– As Mary was so clearly implicated, she was put on trial.*
        *   *– Elizabeth delayed signing the death warrant. (20 marks)*

    (b) The answer should point out the following:
    *   *The outcome of the plots was mainly due to the skill and possible deceptive tactics used by Sir Francis Walsingham.*
    *   *The reluctance of Elizabeth to execute both Norfolk after the Northern Rebellion and Mary, who was involved in all of the plots, shows that she wished to give the impression of magnanimity and tolerance.*

- *Therefore, it can be argued that as the plots did not succeed, and there was no general rising of Roman Catholics, Elizabeth handled the plots well.*
- *However, her reluctance to execute Mary frustrated many of her councillors who felt she had to act more decisively, because they believed her life was in danger.* (10 marks)

3. (a) A good answer should include the following points:
    - *Mary was the daughter of James V, King of Scotland. She became Queen in the same year she was born, due to the death of her father.*
    - *She believed she had a strong claim to the English throne as Henry VIII was her great-uncle.*
    - *Following the suspicious death of her husband, Mary escaped to England.*
    - *She went to her cousin, Elizabeth, but made it clear she felt she had a claim to the throne.*
    - *Elizabeth therefore imprisoned her.*
    - *Mary then planned to marry the Duke of Norfolk, whose family wanted her named as Elizabeth's successor. This led to the Northern Rebellion.*
    - *A second attempt to put Mary on the throne along with the Duke of Norfolk led to the Ridolfi plot.*
    - *Mary then, apparently, wrote to the Spanish Ambassador asking for help in becoming ruler of England. These letters were intercepted by Francis Walsingham's spies.*
    - *Mary then, apparently, wrote to Anthony Babington, calling for Elizabeth to be overthrown by force. As this was treason she was put on trial, found guilty and eventually executed.* (20 marks)

   (b) The answer should include the following points:

    - *The Babington Plot was seen as the last straw.*
    - *The evidence of Mary's direct involvement was clearer than in the other plots, where she could have been seen as naïve or the evidence was rather inconclusive.*
    - *Elizabeth's reluctance to execute Mary was because it would make outright war with Spain inevitable; it would alienate some English Catholics; to execute an anointed sovereign was a very shocking idea, especially to a fellow monarch, regardless of the circumstances.* (10 marks)

Total for exercise: 65 marks

Exercise 4.3

1. *Timeline for the main events that brought England and Spain to war:*

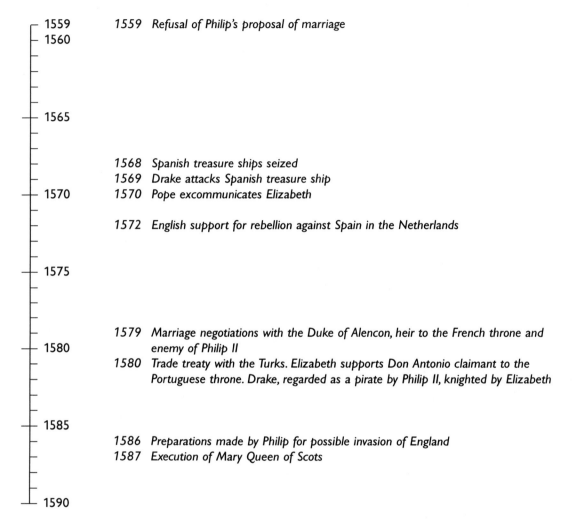

1559	1559 Refusal of Philip's proposal of marriage
1560	
1565	
	1568 Spanish treasure ships seized
	1569 Drake attacks Spanish treasure ship
1570	1570 Pope excommunicates Elizabeth
	1572 English support for rebellion against Spain in the Netherlands
1575	
	1579 Marriage negotiations with the Duke of Alencon, heir to the French throne and
1580	enemy of Philip II
	1580 Trade treaty with the Turks. Elizabeth supports Don Antonio claimant to the
	Portuguese throne. Drake, regarded as a pirate by Philip II, knighted by Elizabeth
1585	
	1586 Preparations made by Philip for possible invasion of England
	1587 Execution of Mary Queen of Scots
1590	

(10 marks)

2. (a) *The reasons for the war between England and Spain include:*

  ● *Religion – Philip saw himself as the champion of Roman Catholicism. Elizabeth was a heretic Queen.*

  ● *The fact that the Pope excommunicated Elizabeth was an official recognition that the duty of Roman Catholics was to overthrow her.*

  ● *There was Spanish involvement in various plots centred on Mary Queen of Scots.*

  ● *For her part, Elizabeth supported Protestant rebels in the Low Countries.*

- Spain was the most powerful European country and Elizabeth wanted to prevent Spain becoming completely dominant. She therefore supported the Dutch rebels and Don Antonio.
- There were trade rivalries on the high seas and attacks on Spanish treasure ships. (20 marks)

(b) On balance the answer should be centred on religion:
- Philip was determined to be a Catholic champion.
- Elizabeth certainly annoyed the Spanish with support for rebels and attacks on Spanish ships, but this can be seen as trying to prevent Spain from becoming so powerful that the Spanish could invade England, depose Elizabeth and restore Catholicism. (10 marks)

3. (a) The following events led to the Spanish Armada in 1588:
- The Pope excommunicated Elizabeth.
- There was increasing tension between England and Spain, possibly due to Elizabeth's earlier refusal to marry Philip II of Spain.
- Mary Queen of Scots was executed and the Spanish had been supportive of the various plots to put Mary on the throne.
- Francis Drake attacked Cadiz and temporarily halted the Spanish invasion plans.
- In 1588 the invasion preparations were complete, with an army of 30,000 in the Netherlands.
- An Armada of 130 ships set sail from Corunna, the plan being to embark the Spanish troops in the Netherlands and launch the invasion of England.
- The fleet under the command of the Duke of Medina Sidonia reached the Channel on 30th July. (20 marks)

(b) The reasons why the Armada was defeated include:
- From the beginning the English had the advantage.
- There was the difficulty of actually embarking Parma's army, and the longer range of the English guns meant that English ships did not have to sail close to the larger Spanish ships and risk being boarded by the troops they carried. As Recalde says, 'the English have faster and handier ships than ours and many more long range guns'.
- The attack by fire ships on 7th August broke up the formation of the Spanish fleet.
- The battle off Gravelines did considerable damage to the Spanish ships and several were lost.
- By the end of this engagement, it was obvious that the Armada would not meet up with Parma's army, so would have to sail home.

- *Storms wrecked many ships already weakened in battle. Sixty ships were lost, of which only four were actually sunk in action.*
- *In conclusion, this was a very risky enterprise. The Armada was fatally weakened by battle damage, but perhaps the final defeat was by the weather. (10 marks)*

Total for exercise: 70 marks

Exercise 4.4

1. (a) *Elizabeth dealt with problems in Ireland by the following:*
   - *Elizabeth imposed a military solution to dealing with Ireland.*
   - *Her most dangerous enemy was Hugh O'Neill, Earl of Tyrone, who had defeated the English at the Battle of Yellow Ford.*
   - *Following this battle, Tyrone was effectively ruling Ireland.*
   - *Elizabeth sent the Earl of Essex to defeat Tyrone but he failed to defeat the rebels in Ireland.*
   - *She then replaced Essex with Lord Mountjoy who was far more competent.*
   - *He defeated Tyrone and his Spanish allies at Kinsale. (20 marks)*

   (b) The following points should be included in the answer:
   - *Ireland had remained Catholic whilst England had become Protestant.*
   - *Thus, many Irish had no love for English royal rule.*
   - *Ireland was a potential backdoor into England for the Spanish, who therefore supported Tyrone's rebellion. (10 marks)*

2. (a) *Elizabeth controlled her Parliaments in the following ways:*
   - *In cases of what Elizabeth saw as outright challenges to her authority she acted decisively.*
   - *She refused to let them put pressure on her to marry.*
   - *Strickland was told very clearly that he was challenging the Royal Prerogative when he tried to effect changes to the Prayer Book.*
   - *Wentworth was actually imprisoned when he criticised Elizabeth.*
   - *On the other hand, she tried to placate Parliament as much as possible in order to avoid conflict.*
   - *She also knew she needed Parliament in order to pass laws and raise taxes.*
   - *The Golden Speech of 1601 summed up her desire to act with Parliament, 'I have reigned with your loves'. (20 marks)*

   (b) *Overall, Elizabeth was successful in her dealings with Parliament:*
   - *She was able to defend the Royal Prerogative over religion, the succession and foreign affairs, by acting decisively when MPs challenged her authority in these areas.*

- *Strickland was told very clearly that he was challenging the Royal Prerogative when he tried to effect changes to the Prayer Book.*
- *Wentworth was actually imprisoned when he criticised Elizabeth.*
- *However, she resented the fact that she was dependent on Parliament in order to raise taxes and there were signs of increasing strain in the relationship between the Crown and Parliament towards the end of her reign, particularly in the area of finance.* (10 marks)

3. (a)

Successes/strengths	Failures/shortcomings
She was successful in dealing with the threat posed by Spain.	The essential problem of Ireland was not solved despite the defeat of O'Neill.
Her relations with Parliament, despite some frictions, remained good.	The succession was left open.
The Elizabethan Settlement of the Church was one that the majority of English people could accept.	The 1590s were a period of acute hardship for many of the poor.
She was excellent at public relations.	Many of the problems of the last years were left to be dealt with by her successor.
The Poor Law at least provided a basis for helping the poorest in society and survived for another two hundred years.	

(20 marks)

(b) This question can be answered in a number of ways and pupils should include supporting evidence for their choice. Some historians would point to the durability of the Elizabethan Settlement, whilst others would emphasise the clever diplomatic manoeuvres that prevented all-out war with Spain for nearly twenty years. Parliament had become, perhaps, more self-confident and assertive, and she managed to control these forces through a mixture of charm and firmness.

Therefore, an answer that can put forward the case for any of the above with supporting evidence must be accepted and rewarded.

On the matter of the title of 'Good Queen Bess', the answer should quote from the Golden speech, whilst realising that it can be seen as a form of propaganda. For some Catholics, Elizabeth is certainly not Good Queen Bess, and answers should at least be aware of that. Given the position of women in the 16th century, an answer that is aware of Elizabeth's great achievement as a woman to be a successful monarch in a male-dominated society should also be rewarded. (10 marks)

4. The following points should be included in the answer:
   - *This is another example of royal propaganda. It is how the Queen would have liked to see herself.*
   - *The star symbolism is important; the Queen is seen as far above her subjects in the heavens.*
   - *The star image implies that the Queen is depicted as Astraea, the star-maiden, which is also related to virginity, Virgo.*
   - *The image of virginity is further emphasised by the pearl decoration. The implication is not only that the Queen is a virgin, but that she is married to her country only.*
   - *Her wisdom is pointed out by the serpent, which represents wisdom.*
   - *She is portrayed as the bringer of peace with an olive branch in her hand and a sheathed sword.*
   - *She is painted as being younger than she is, implying that she is unchanging and therefore almost above mortality; it is also a piece of flattery in keeping with the exalted view of the monarchy and assumed female vanity.*
   - *Her clothing shows her regal status.* (20 marks)

Answers may well draw out other inferences.

5. (a) *Elizabeth addressed the problems she faced in the following ways:*
   - *The succession. She postponed a decision on this and refused to be bullied by Parliament on the matter, and, in the end, never married.*
   - *Religion. She created a tolerant broad Church in the hope of satisfying both moderate Catholics and Protestants in the 1559 Settlement, which was successful. Only fanatical Catholics and Puritans did not accept it; most English people did.*
   - *Foreign policy. There were threats from France at the beginning of her reign and then Spain. Both were dealt with.*
   - *Finance. The Crown was poor, and she had to go continually to Parliament for money.*

- As far as the problem of the poor was concerned, the Elizabethan Poor Laws were passed. (20 marks)

(b) This question is open to debate and pupils should back up their answers with evidence. A possible answer could include the following:
- The succession problem was eventually dealt with by postponement until a time when it was obvious that she would never marry and produce an heir.
- The 1559 Settlement can be seen as durable, tolerant and sensible. Only the extreme Catholics and Puritans found themselves unable to accept it.
- Foreign policy was, again, skilfully handled, partly due to good fortune, partly her ability to prolong negotiations and prevent all-out war. After the execution of Mary Queen of Scots, Elizabeth had to reckon with all-out hostility from Philip II.
- Finance was a difficult matter for Elizabeth. Inflation in the 1590s, not perhaps her fault, and the poverty of the Crown were serious problems. The poor suffered considerably and Parliament became rather weary of granting further taxation. This issue was never really resolved. (10 marks)

Total for exercise: 140 marks

Chapter 5 Life in the 16th century

Exercise 5.1

1.

Causes of enclosure	Process of enclosure	Results of enclosure
Landowners turning to sheep farming rather than arable	Former open fields enclosed by walls and hedges to stop sheep roaming	Cause of resentment and hardship to poorer people
Wool trade more lucrative	Common land, used by everyone in the village, fenced off	Loss of jobs on the land
Sheep farming less labour intensive		Could not grow own corn or vegetables
Land needed to be enclosed for the sheep		Unable to graze own animals and poultry for free
		More money raised in taxes due to increase in wool exports

(10 marks)

(a) *There were two types of enclosure:*
  - *The first type was the enclosure of former open fields.*
    - *Walls or hedges enclosed these, so that the far more profitable sheep farming could be conducted without the sheep roaming.*
    - *Sheep were more profitable than arable farming because of demand for wool and the fact that pasture needed fewer workers.*
  - *The second type was the enclosure of the common land.*
    - *This was fencing off of land that had previously been used by everyone in the village to graze their animals and keep their poultry.* (20 marks)

(b) *Enclosure was a source of great resentment and hardship to the poorer people in the 16th century:*
  - *The enclosure for pasture meant a loss of jobs on the land.*

- *The loss of the open fields meant that many could not grow their own corn or vegetables.*
- *The loss of the common land was, perhaps, even more important. No longer could ordinary people graze their animals and poultry for nothing. They needed these animals and poultry in order to provide food to survive through the hard winter months.*
- *These factors caused severe hardship for the poor.*
- *The reaction of many was to protest or revolt.* (10 marks)

Total for exercise: 40 marks

Exercise 5.2

1. (a) *London merchants prospered during the 16th century. Cloth became the most important export, rather than raw wool. They found new products to sell from South America and the Indies.* (2 marks)

   (b) *Joint stock companies sold shares to landowners to reduce the risk of loss. The government offered these companies a monopoly in trade to new countries.* (2 marks)

   (c) *The East India Company was founded as a challenge to the Dutch monopoly in the spice trade. It was granted a charter in 1600 and soon broke the Dutch control of the trade in spices.* (2 marks)

   (d) *Antwerp had been the main import and export centre in the 16th century, but, in 1576, it was destroyed by the Spanish during the 'Revolt of the Netherlands'. This helped the rise of London.* (2 marks)

Total for exercise: 8 marks

Exercise 5.3

The reasons for the growth in trade, in order of importance:
- *There was a trade boom from 1560 due to growth of exports of finished cloth.*
- *Other industries developed.*
- *London merchants exported goods from the New World and the east.*
- *Joint stock companies were formed such as the East India Company.*
- *Antwerp was destroyed.*
- *Other ports became important, such as Bristol and Liverpool.* (5 marks)

(a) A good answer should include the following points:
- *Trade expanded in the 16th century due to changes in the economy.*
- *It changed from trade in agriculture to trade in manufactured goods.*
- *New industries such as iron, coal, copper, lead and salt developed.*
- *England was able to benefit from the booming trade in Europe.*
- *Cloth exports grew.*
- *New markets were found abroad.*
- *Goods from the east were imported into London and re-exported.*
- *Joint stock companies were formed and these companies were offered a monopoly in trade to new countries.* (20 marks)

(b) *The reasons for the growth in trade include:*
- *The Rise in the population in Europe and demand for goods created a trade boom.*
- *Antwerp was the centre of European trade, far more important than London. With its destruction in 1576, the way was open for London merchants to seize Antwerp's import/export trade.*
- *Merchants became more sophisticated in their operations and the development of joint stock companies provided new capital.*
- *English ships were sailing to the New World and the east, bringing back valuable cargo.*
- *The East India Company was able to break the monopoly of the Dutch in the spice trade.* (10 marks)

Total for exercise: 35 marks

Exercise 5.4

1. (a) *The reasons for inflation in the 16th century were:*
   - *Population growth.*
   - *Debasement of the coinage.*
   - *Increased government spending.*
   - *Bad harvests.*
   - *Land sales.* (5 marks)

   (b) Answers could include either of these links:
   - *There are links between debasement of the coinage and increased government spending. Governments were very short of money and debasement was a quick, if damaging, solution to their problem.*

● *It could be said that population growth might not have had such an effect if goods and food production could have kept up. Bad harvests ensured it did not.* (5 marks)

(c) *Probably the most important single factor with regard to inflation was population growth. With an increase in population of possibly 1.2 million without any significant improvements in agriculture, prices of food were bound to go up. This led to there being 10,000 beggars.* (5 marks)

2. (a) *Overseers were responsible for collecting the Poor Rate and distributing it to the poor. There were two Overseers of the Poor in each parish.* (2 marks)

(b) *The idle poor were those who were able to work but chose not to. They were regarded as undeserving of any charity.* (2 marks)

(c) *The deserving poor were those unable to work through illness or disability or were poor because they were widowed, for example. They received money from the Poor Rate.* (2 marks)

(d) *Indoor relief was help given to the deserving poor living in a parish poorhouse.* (2 marks)

(e) *Outdoor relief was charity given to the deserving poor in their own home.* (2 marks)

(f) *Poorhouses were built in some parishes. All the deserving poor were fed and housed there.* (2 marks)

3. This answer should be very clear as to the difference between the attitude of the authorities towards the poor, dependent on whether they were seen as idle or deserving: deserving received Parish relief or shelter in the poorhouse; undeserving received punishment such as whipping, branding, sending to a House of Correction (hard labour in prison conditions) and even the threat of death. (10 marks)

Total for exercise: 37 marks

Exercise 5.5

1. (a) A good answer should include the following points:
   ● *The Poor Laws meant there was a distinction between the idle poor and deserving poor.*
   ● *The idle poor were those who were able to work but chose not to. They were regarded as undeserving of any charity.*

- *The deserving poor were those unable to work through illness or disability or were poor because they were widowed, for example. They received money from the Poor Rate.*
- *The Poor Rate was collected from the rich by Overseers of the Poor, who then distributed it to the deserving poor.*
- *In some parishes poorhouses were built and the deserving poor were housed and fed there.*
- *If there was no poorhouse, the deserving poor would receive outdoor relief, which meant they would receive help in their own home.*
- *The idle poor would be whipped and sent back to the parish where they were born if they were found begging in a different parish.*
- *If they continued to beg they would be sent to a House of Correction or hanged.* (20 marks)

(b) *The treatment of the poor was unfair because:*
- *Unemployment could be unavoidable in trade depressions and hard times.*
- *The dissolution of the monasteries removed any chance of local people finding work there.*
- *Monks and nuns now had to find work, despite having no experience of many jobs.*
- *Some able-bodied poor who simply could not find work were punished as undeserving poor.* (10 marks)

2. The diagram should include the links between bad harvests and unemployment, the dissolution of the monasteries and the fall in charitable giving, inflation and bad harvests leading to further unemployment. (5 marks)

3. Answers could include the following points:
- *It might be hard to diagnose illness so someone who looked fit and able to work might actually be ill.*
- *In hard times, able-bodied people found themselves out of work through no fault of their own. They were still classed as undeserving.* (5 marks)

Total for exercise: 45 marks

Exercise 5.6

1. (a) *A typical Tudor town would have the following:*
- *Narrow unpaved streets and tall houses.*
- *No sewers or waste collection.*

- Different areas given over to different trades. For example, in London, the street names tell us where certain trades were carried out.
- Water from pumps or wells.
- Many Tudor towns grew rapidly. For example, in London the population rose from 60,000 to 250,000.

A good answer should include some example street names for the various trades and population figures. (20 marks)

(b) Life in a typical Tudor town was likely to be unhealthy because:
- There was no sewage disposal.
- The rivers were polluted and there were polluted water supplies.
- People crowded very close together. (10 marks)

2. (a) The most common forms of entertainment included:
- Dancing.
- Music and singing – in rich households the whole family played instruments such as the lute, viol, flute, virginal or spinet.
- Hunting, bowls, archery, real tennis, football.
- Bear-baiting and cock-fighting.
- The theatre also grew in popularity. (20 marks)

(b) To an extent this answer will depend on individual likes and dislikes and, as such, reasoning will be the important factor. It would be expected that violent football, bear-baiting and cock-fighting would be unpopular but unconventional answers, if reasoned, are acceptable. (10 marks)

3. (a) Poor people living in towns lived in the following conditions:
- Their home would be a hut with only one or two rooms.
- There would be no proper chimney.
- Their beds would be mattresses stuffed with straw, usually put straight onto the hard earth.
- Furniture would be very basic, perhaps benches, stools, a table and a wooden chest.
- Water would be collected from a common well.
- They would have lived in very unsanitary conditions as there were no proper sewers or drains. (20 marks)

(b) The government tried to help the poor in the following ways:
- The government enacted the Poor Law. Through this, those poor who were old, cold or infirm and could not work were given assistance.

- There were two forms of parish help: outdoor relief, where money collected from the richer members of the parish was given to the poor in their own homes, or indoor relief, where they were given shelter in the poorhouse, where they were fed and clothed.
- The government was not interested in helping the able-bodied, idle poor. They were whipped and made to work. (10 marks)

Total for exercise: 90 marks

Exercise 5.7

1. (a) The life of a poor woman differed from that of a rich woman in the following ways:
    - Poor women were expected to do manual labour.
    - They would work in the fields, spin wool or mend clothes.
    - They would work from dawn to dusk.
    - They were also expected to look after the children and cook the meals.
    - Rich women had servants to do the housework.
    - According to a visitor to England in 1575 'they spend time walking, playing cards and visiting friends'.
    - However, rich women were expected to ensure that the servants did their tasks properly so that everything was right for when the husband returned to the house. (20 marks)

    (b) The answer should contain the following points:
    - The visitor is comparing the life of English women who are rich to those abroad.
    - Marriages were frequently arranged and were not love matches.
    - Childbirth was extremely dangerous and many women died in or shortly after giving birth due to the lack of hygiene.
    - They were not necessarily well educated; even some rich women could not read or write properly.
    - Poor women were even worse off; they had a life of drudgery.
    - The position of women in the 16th century was not enviable and very different to that of women today. (10 marks)

2. (a)

	Women in the 16th century	Women today
Marriage	Arranged	For love
Education	Limited	Same as men
Childbirth	Very dangerous; no contraception; frequent pregnancies	Safe; planned childbirth
Legal rights	Very few; property belonged to husband; adultery severely punished even by death	Legal equality with men
Employment	In the home only; poor women help others with menial jobs	Legal equality with men; any work open to women

(20 marks)

(b) The answer to this question could pick out any of the points in relation to marriage, education, childbirth or legal rights. A good answer should be backed up by supporting evidence. (10 marks)

Total for exercise: 60 marks

Exercise 5.8

1. Source A shows that women were expected to do some of the hardest work if required in time of need. Haymaking, muck cart driving, ploughing, selling produce at market were all women's tasks. (2 marks)

2. Source B suggests, unlike Source A, that women could live a life of leisure, 'stroll round or drive out by coach'. It also suggests that women were the equal of men who had to 'put up with such behaviour'. It even suggests that women 'often beat their men'. (3 marks)

3. The following points should be included in the answer:
   - Source C shows a rich woman.
   - Her clothes, the fact that she is playing a musical instrument and her jewellery all suggest wealth.
   - Source A is referring to poor women or farmers' wives, not the woman in the picture of Source C.

- *Therefore, Source C does not support Source A because they are about women from very different social classes. (7 marks)*

4. A good answer should make reference to each of the sources and should include the following points:
   - *The majority of women in the 16th century were not rich. Therefore, Source B and Source C refer to a minority.*
   - *Source B may contain some exaggeration, especially 'the good wives often beat their men'. This does not bear out the very weak legal position of women at that time, so is probably inaccurate or an untypical situation which was observed by the writer.*
   - *Both in law and as far as the teachings of the Church were concerned, women were definitely regarded as inferior to men: 'the weaker vessel'.*
   - *Arranged marriages meant that women had no choice over their husbands, so again Source B seems to be exaggerated.*
   - *Source A gives a good picture of the life of the majority of women in the 16th century, so is the most accurate. Sources B and C refer to a very small minority, and for most women life was not like that portrayed in B and C. (8 marks)*

Total for exercise: 20 marks

Chapter 6 James I and Charles I

Exercise 6.1

1. This is an exercise in imagination but good answers should include the
    following points:
    - The names of the conspirators.
    - What they were setting out to do and how.
    - Details regarding the Monteagle letter.
    - The arrest of Guy Fawkes and the rapid round-up of the other conspirators.

    It should be clear why Catholics might wish to destroy James and Parliament.
    (10 marks)

2. (a) The answer should include the following points:
    - *The Hampton Court conference destroyed any hopes that Catholics would have had of religious tolerance.*
    - *The new session of Parliament was due to open on 5th November 1605.*
    - *A plot was devised by Catesby and Percy which involved putting gunpowder under the House of Commons in a cellar they had rented.*
    - *Francis Tresham warned his brother in law, Lord Monteagle, not to attend the opening of Parliament: 'devise some excuse to shift your attendance at this Parliament'.*
    - *Monteagle gave the letter to Robert Cecil.*
    - *The cellars beneath Parliament were searched on 4th November and this led to the arrest of Guy Fawkes. (20 marks)*

    (b) *The Gunpowder Plot worked in James's favour in the following ways:*
    - *The plot would have been seen as showing that Catholics could not be trusted; they were all potential traitors.*
    - *James's government could have encouraged this feeling by spreading anti-Catholic propaganda.*
    - *By having narrowly escaped assassination, James could encourage people to think that he was protected by God.*
    - *The overall impression would have been that James's Protestantism was the true belief, compared with the Catholic plots which God caused to fail. (10 marks)*

3. *The source is useful in the following ways:*
    - *The letter suggests that the government actually were, in some way, trying to trap Catholics into acts of treachery: 'foul play', 'secretly spun a web'.*

- *The source is written by an Italian Catholic, so he is likely to be biased in favour of fellow Catholics and therefore the source must be treated with caution.*
- *It does not actually give any indications as to why the government should wish to mistreat Catholics, or why the Gunpowder plotters were hanged, drawn and quartered.*
- *It is useful to indicate, perhaps, how some Catholics felt about the Plot.* (10 marks)

Total for exercise: 50 marks

Exercise 6.2

1. There will obviously be huge variety in answers here and markers should use their own valuation, knowledge and initiative on this question. (10 marks)

2. *Richard III is portrayed as an evil tyrant for the following reasons:*
   - *Shakespeare was writing with the approval of the King in mind.*
   - *Richard was deposed and killed by Henry VII.*
   - *James's claim to the throne came through the connection with the Tudors, so the deposition of Richard gave not only Elizabeth but also James legitimacy.*
   (10 marks)

Total for exercise: 20 marks

Exercise 6.3

1. *Source A shows that James's court was very extravagant. The excess and waste is shown by the fact that a guest would be faced with a wonderful feast that was then thrown away before another hot meal was produced. A lot of food was taken home.* (2 marks)

2. *Weldon's account of James supports Source A. It shows James as spendthrift and lavish. Weldon writes that James 'spent much', and Osbourne claims that he is 'cloyed with the repetition of this excess'.* (3 marks)

3. The answer should include the following points:
   - *Both sources give a picture of irresponsibility and extravagance.*
   - *Source A is more specific about money: 'he spent much', 'he was very liberal'. It implies that James spent money he did not have rather than his own money.*
   - *This would inevitably lead to financial difficulties.* (7 marks)

4. The answer should cover some of the points below:
   - James's troubles with Parliament were partly the result of finance. As the two sources show, he was extravagant and lacking in financial sense. Parliament objected to having to grant him extra money, which they thought he would just waste.
   - His shortage of money caused further friction because he sold peerages (titles of honour) and monopolies.
   - There were other reasons for frictions with Parliament.
   - Buckingham, the King's favourite, was very unpopular. He sold offices (posts within the government) and monopolies. In 1621, Parliament attacked Buckingham's conduct.
   - Parliament wished to discuss foreign policy and was worried about the possibility of Charles's marriage to a Roman Catholic Spanish princess, the Infanta.
   - James opposed war with Spain in 1624, as did Cranfield, the Lord Treasurer. Parliament attacked Cranfield, impeaching him and granted money for war with Spain, a war that was being encouraged by Charles and Buckingham.
   - Parliament was suspicious of the doctrine of the Divine Right of Kings, which James believed in: 'Kings are the makers of laws' and 'It is contempt in a subject to say that a King cannot do this or that'.
   - There was concern in Parliament that James wished to rule without reference to it. (8 marks)

Total for exercise: 20 marks

Exercise 6.4

1. (a) The main problems facing James were:
   - Crown finances.
   - Religion: some Puritans wanted a more Protestant/Calvinist church without bishops; Catholics hoped for toleration.
   - James's view on the constitution: the Divine Right of Kings.
   - Foreign policy.
   - An unpopular favourite Buckingham.

   Connections can be made between fear of Catholics and a pro-Catholic foreign policy (marriage to the Infanta), and the Puritan leanings of many of James's subjects; finance and the Duke of Buckingham, sale of offices/monopolies; the Divine Right of Kings and James's view that certain matters should not be discussed by Parliament – this included foreign policy and religion. (10 marks)

(b) This is still a matter of debate amongst historians, so any answer that gives a clear well-reasoned response can be accepted. The sample answer below puts finance at the top of the list:

- *Finance was the most important issue because James was perpetually short of money. He therefore had to call Parliaments.*
- *He then clashed with these Parliaments on other issues: the Divine Right of Kings, religion, foreign policy, role of favourites.*
- *Buckingham was a particular problem, whilst James eventually dealt quite well with religion, despite the dissatisfaction of the Catholic minority.*
- *Therefore, a possible ranking would be: finance, Buckingham, Divine Right, foreign policy, religion.* (10 marks)

2. (a) The answer should include the following points:
- *Parliament initially welcomed James.*
- *It soon became apparent that he was a spendthrift and expected Parliament to give him extra money.*
- *He sold titles of honour, offices and monopolies to get money, all of which angered Parliament.*
- *James increasingly took advice from his favourite Buckingham, 'you may be sure I love the Duke of Buckingham more than anyone else, and more than you who are here assembled', which was very much resented by Parliament.*
- *James's speeches to Parliament about the Divine Right of Kings made members very uneasy.*
- *The 1614 Parliament was dismissed because it failed to grant James the money he wanted, whilst the 1621 Parliament, angered by Buckingham's power over the King and by the pro-Spanish foreign policy, clashed with James to such an extent that he dismissed it.*
- *1624 was more harmonious with the impeachment of Cranfield.* (20 marks)

(b) A good answer will include the following points:
- *James's lack of financial sense soon caused problems. In theory, the monarch should not have asked Parliament for money in peace time.*
- *The court was regarded as expensive and corrupt. MPs objected to paying for this conspicuous consumption of 'dishes, as high as a tall man'.*
- *James was insensitive in his dealings with Parliament, insisting on the Divine Right of Kings, when tact was required.*
- *The Duke of Buckingham, described by one MP as the 'grievance of grievances', became the most hated man in the country. MPs believed he had total power and influence over James and he used this to enrich himself.*

- *Significantly, despite some irritations, Elizabeth had got on well with her Parliaments, whilst a gap opened up between the monarch and Parliament during James's reign. (10 marks)*

3. (a) *James's attitude to religion was as follows:*
   - *James was basically very tolerant of religion.*
   - *James was a Protestant but not a Puritan and he refused to introduce more radical forms of Protestantism.*
   - *He, at first, hoped to help Catholics, although he reconsidered this following the Main Plot and the Bye Plot.*
   - *He also continued Elizabeth's policy of appealing to as wide a body of the Church as he could.*
   - *He was well educated and interested in Biblical studies.*
   - *He commissioned another translation of the Bible into English. (20 marks)*

   (b) *James's attitude created problems in the following ways:*
   - *James, at first, did try to help Catholics – posts were given to Catholic noblemen (Northumberland and Northampton) and recusancy fines were abolished.*
   - *Catholic hopes were raised but not fulfilled, and the result was the Gunpowder Plot, after which Catholics were again persecuted.*
   - *He hoped also to appease the Puritans by calling the Hampton Court Conference. The Conference was a failure as the Puritan demands, including the abolition of bishops, were too much for James. Some extreme Puritans decided to emigrate.*
   - *James was in an impossible position in the early years of his reign, a position that was not his fault, except that he may have raised hopes that could not be fulfilled. (10 marks)*

   It could also be argued that the Divine Right of Kings can be seen as a religious belief or attitude which caused problems with Parliament.

   Total for exercise: 80 marks

Exercise 6.5

1. (a) *Forced loans were demands for money from Charles that he resorted to when Parliament would not grant him enough money. (2 marks)*

   (b) *The king always collected fines for law-breaking, so he revived old laws to raise money. (2 marks)*

    (c) *Monopolies were the sole right to trade in a certain area or in a particular commodity.* (2 marks)

    (d) *Coastal counties had always paid for ships to protect the county, but Charles extended ship money to all counties.* (2 marks)

2.   Any answer should contain the following points:
- There was justification by Divine Right.
- The assertion that Parliament had not co-operated with him.
- That forced loans were legal. (5 marks)

3.   (a) *Clarendon regarded personal rule as:*
- *A time of peace and prosperity.*
- *A time of happiness and calm*
- *He believed Laud had strengthened the Protestant religion, as it was understood in the Church of England.* (5 marks)

    (b) The answer should contain the following points in relation to Source A:
- *Source A is contemporary; Clarendon lived through the events he describes.*
- *This gives the source some real historical value.*
- *However, Clarendon was a Royalist and supported Charles I during the Civil War, as well as being chief minister for the first few years of Charles II's reign, so some caution is needed.* (5 marks)

                       Total for exercise: 23 marks

Exercise 6.6

1.   (a) *Charles's relations with the Church were as follows:*
- *Charles disliked Puritans.*
- *He believed in the Divine Right of Kings and therefore his authority over the Church could not be challenged.*
- *In 1633 Laud was appointed Archbishop of Canterbury. Laud's beliefs were the same as Charles's.*
- *Laud believed in the power of bishops, ceremonies and decoration of churches, 'the beauty of holiness'.*
- *Charles and Laud agreed that Puritans such as Burton, Payne and Bastwick should be severely punished.*
- *They worked for conformity in Church services and practices.* (20 marks)

(b) Charles's views brought him into conflict with Scotland for the following reasons:

- Charles was a high church Anglican; the Scots were Puritans and Presbyterians.
- Charles was determined to force the new Laudian Prayer Book on the Scots and give five bishops in Scotland more power. Many Scots were opposed to bishops; others certainly did not want them to have any more powers.
- The Scots then rebelled, determined to defend their Presbyterian church.
(10 marks)

2. (a) Laud faced the following opposition while Archbishop of Canterbury:

- Opposition came from Puritans.
- Burton, Prynne, Bastwick and John Lilburne opposed his attempts at uniformity of worship and were all punished.
- The Scots opposed Laud because of his attempt to destroy their Presbyterian church.
- Puritans in Parliament opposed him.
- Both Scots and Puritans believed Laud was a secret Roman Catholic.
(20 marks)

(b) Laud's actions led to his beheading for the following reasons:

- Laud was seen by his Puritan opponents as bringing in Roman Catholicism with his ceremonies.
- He was seen as responsible for the two Bishops' Wars by trying to introduce a new Prayer Book.
- The English were defeated at the First Bishops' War, which led to Laud being accused of treason, imprisoned and beheaded. (10 marks)

Total for exercise: 60 marks

Exercise 6.7

1. The correct dates and order are as follows:

First Bishops' War	1639
Short Parliament	May 1640
Second Bishops' War	October 1640
Long Parliament	November 1640
Trial of Strafford	March 1641 (5 marks)

2. Parliament had the following grievances:
   - Charles had dismissed Parliament before the complaints had been heard.
   - He had imprisoned MPs for speaking freely.
   - Pym believed that Roman Catholicism was being introduced.
   - It was felt that property was not safe under the King, who was taking taxes without the legal right to do so. (10 marks)

3.

Political reasons	Economic reasons	Religious reasons
Charles's belief in the Divine Right	Forced loans	Belief that Charles and Archbishop Laud were intent on bringing in Roman Catholicism and destroying the Church of England
Charles's decision to rule without Parliament – the Eleven Year Tyranny	Monopolies	The rise of Puritanism
Charles's clashes with Parliament in 1641	Ship money	
	Fines	

(10 marks)

(a) The reasons for the conflict between Charles and Parliament were as follows:
   - There was a fundamental difference of opinion between Parliament and the King over the rights of the subjects and the rights of the monarch.
   - In particular, they disagreed on the rights of the King to levy forced loans, levy ship money and imprison MPs.
   - Charles believed in the Divine Right of Kings and, as such, did not need to bow to or consider Parliament's wishes.
   - With the introduction of Laud's religious changes, it made many people think that Roman Catholicism was being introduced.
   - Many Puritans became increasingly self-confident.
   - There were clashes between Charles and Parliament in 1641 over Strafford and Parliament's demands.

- Charles, under pressure from Parliament, reluctantly agreed to these demands.
- The demands consisted of Parliaments being called every three years; abolition of ship money and monopolies; punishment of unpopular ministers; abolition of the Star Chamber; Parliament was not to be dismissed by the King, only Parliament could vote for its own dismissal. (20 marks)

(b) A good answer should refer to the difference in opinion regarding the Divine Right of Kings, the fact that many people thought that Catholicism was being introduced and the demands put forward by Parliament, which led to a situation of crisis in 1641, with Charles on one side and Parliament on the other. The answer should stress that Charles and Parliament had fundamental disagreements about the constitution and religion that were very hard to reconcile. (10 marks)

Total for exercise: 55 marks

Exercise 6.8

It should be stressed that the causes of the Civil War and, in particular, the events of 1640–1642, have been the subject of a great deal of historical controversy and that several answers and interpretations can be seen as valid. This is taken into account in the following answers:

1. (a) The Nineteen Propositions consisted of the following:
   - Parliament would approve the appointment of the King's ministers.
   - Parliament would have to agree to all affairs of state.
   - The recusancy laws against Catholics must be enforced.
   - Church reform would be undertaken with Parliament's approval.
   - Parliament would control the army.

   N.B. Pupils should be encouraged to read all the Nineteen Propositions, as one MP described them as 'the principal foundation of the ensuing war'. (20 marks)

   (b) The Nineteen Propositions were not supported by some MPs because:
   - They changed the constitution, as control of the army and the choosing of ministers had always been the right ('prerogative') of the monarch.
   - Some MPs were only moderate Protestants and not fanatical Puritans.
   - There was unease that Parliament might reform the Church of England too radically by getting rid of bishops, or even completely abolishing the Church. (10 marks)

2. (a)

Beliefs and actions of Charles I	Beliefs and actions of MPs
Beliefs:	**Beliefs:**
Divine right	Many were Puritans, and most did not like Laud
Laud's changes to the Church with Charles's support	Distrusted Charles and his advisers
	Did not accept the Divine Right
	Did not accept Charles's right to collect taxation without Parliamentary consent
Actions:	**Actions:**
Collected taxes without Parliamentary consent	Impeached and executed Strafford
Ruled without Parliament for eleven years	Imprisoned Laud (later executed)
Imprisoned his opponents	Drew up the Nineteen Propositions
Attempted to arrest the five MPs	
Refused to accept the Nineteen Propositions	

(10 marks)

(b) N.B. It should be noted that the Irish Rebellion is vital in the causation of the Civil War because it brought into sharp focus the fundamental question: could the King be trusted? If he were granted command of the army would he use it to put down Parliament or the Irish rebels? Pym and his supporters thought the former and this belief was strengthened by the Five Members' coup in January 1642.

Long-term causes	Short-term causes	Triggers
Charles's belief in the Divine Right	Bishops' Wars meant Parliament had to be called because Charles had no money, this meant the end of personal rule	Attempted arrest of the five MPs
Taxation without Parliamentary consent	Clashes between Charles and Pym's supporters in Parliament over punishment of the King's ministers and reduction of the King's powers	King left London
Laud's changes to the Church	Radical religious demands by some MPs (abolition of bishops)	The Nineteen Propositions
The rise of Puritanism	The rebellion in Ireland created the final crisis	Charles raised his standard, declared war on Parliament
The Eleven Year Tyranny (personal rule)		

(10 marks)

3. (a) The answer should cover the following points:
   - Charles had problems with money from the beginning of his reign.
   - Parliament in 1627 refused to grant him all the money he needed.
   - Increases in custom duties led to the Petition of Right, 'no tax shall be laid or levied by the King ... without the goodwill and assent of Parliament'.

- *The Three Resolutions led to the King dismissing Parliament and he ruled by personal rule for eleven years.*
- *Although Parliament was recalled in 1640 after the Scottish (Bishops') Wars, Parliament still continued to quarrel with Charles over his ministers, finance and religion.*
- *Charles believed in the Divine Right of Kings but his Parliament did not.*
- *Charles believed he had the right to collect taxes without Parliamentary consent.*
- *Charles supported Laud's changes to the Church but Parliament thought this was a return to Catholicism.* (20 marks)

(b) The answer should stress the importance of Divine Right beliefs of both Charles and James. These seemed to, or did, challenge the rights of Parliament.
- *Neither James nor Charles was tactful with Parliament.*
- *Some MPs wanted Parliament to be more powerful.*
- *Some were strong Puritans who wished to change the Church of England; neither James nor Charles would accept that.*
- *Between 1640 and 1642 relations broke down totally, with Charles trying to arrest five MPs, followed by Parliament passing the Nineteen Propositions.* (10 marks)

4. (a) *Charles's attitude towards religion was as follows:*
- *Charles believed in the Divine Right of Kings.*
- *This meant that he believed that God had appointed him King and, therefore, he could not be challenged.*
- *Charles was deeply religious*
- *He supported the high church changes to the Church of England put forward by Laud.*
- *This favoured ceremony and lavish ornamentation in the services and placed a high degree of importance on the role of bishops and priests.*
- *He viewed the Puritans with dislike and suspicion.* (20 marks)

(b) The answer should include the following points:
- *The Catholics themselves were not a problem for Charles, but the fact that many Puritans thought his Archbishop of Canterbury, William Laud, was a secret Catholic, and Charles's Catholic wife Henrietta Maria was believed to have great influence over him, was a problem.*

- The Puritans were a greater problem because they had a strong group in Parliament led by Pym and they were determined to stop Laud's religious policies. (10 marks)

Total for exercise: 110 marks

Exercise 6.9

1. It refers to the Star Chamber, a royal prerogative court which no one but the monarch had any control over. (2 marks)

2. Source B presents Charles as a reasonable monarch who was flexible and tried to come to an agreement with the Long Parliament.

N.B. This source from a present-day historian can be seen to be biased. There is considerable debate about this interpretation. Many historians see Charles only consenting to the measures listed under pressure. The source should be used with great caution. (3 marks)

3. Source C is not particularly useful to a historian because:
   - It dates from about 200 years after the events it portrays.
   - It presents a romantic view of both Charles and Parliament. It shows both sides as dignified, but does give an impression of Charles as haughty and Parliament as shocked.
   - As source material it is very limited but is accurate as to dress. (7 marks)

4. The answer should include the following:
   - Source A gives a good impression of how some members of Parliament saw Charles's government as a form of tyranny.
   - Source B gives a different impression: Charles is portrayed as flexible and reasonable.
   - Source C is a Victorian representation of the attempted arrest of the five MPs and is a work of the imagination, but it does show a very important stage on the road to Civil War.

   After this the answer is, again, a matter of debate. A very good answer will provide balance and stress that both sides had points in their favour.
   - Charles can be seen as defending his rights by refusing the Nineteen Propositions because they were, in terms of the 17th century constitution, a fundamental change and an attack on his right.
   - Pym and his followers distrusted Charles, and had memories of previous illegal policies.

- *The attempted arrest of the five MPs was a disastrous mistake by Charles. Many would conclude that it only confirmed the worst suspicions of Pym and his followers and led to Civil War.*

N.B. It should be noted that many wished to remain neutral in the Civil War as they distrusted Charles and disliked Laud's changes to the Church, but thought that Pym and his followers in Parliament were going too far. Only ten per cent of the gentry fought for either side in the Civil War. (8 marks)

Total for exercise: 20 marks

Chapter 7 Civil War and the republican experiment

Exercise 7.1

1. (a) *The Battle of Edgehill took place in October 1642. The Royalist cavalry did well but battle ended as a stalemate. The King failed to advance on London and lost his best chance of winning the war quickly.* (3 marks)

   (b) *The Battle of Marston Moor took place in July 1644. This was a very important battle. The Royalists were commanded by Prince Rupert; the Parliamentary troops were commanded by Sir Thomas Fairfax and Oliver Cromwell. After initial Royalist successes, Cromwell's cavalry (Ironsides) broke the Royalist infantry. The Royalist defeat meant that the King lost control over the north of England.* (4 marks)

   (c) *The Battle of Naseby took place in June 1645. It was the first battle of the New Model Army. Rupert charged too quickly and then Cromwell's cavalry struck, crushing Royalist infantry. With the Royalists defeated, this was the last great pitched battle of the first Civil War.* (3 marks)

2. (a) *Sir Thomas Fairfax was partly responsible for Parliamentary victory at Marston Moor. He became commander of the New Model Army in 1644.* (3 marks)

   (b) *Prince Rupert was an inspiring leader of cavalry who made a name for himself as a daring commander. However, he failed to control his cavalry in the large battles such as Marston Moor and Naseby. Unlike Cromwell, he did not train his cavalry to rein up after a charge so they tended not to return to the battlefield in an organised manner.* (4 marks)

   (c) *Oliver Cromwell raised a cavalry for Parliament. He insisted on strict discipline; his cavalry earned the name Ironsides. This was vital in securing victory for Parliament at Marston Moor and Naseby.* (3 marks)

3. Even though this is a work of imagination, the answer should contain the following points:
   - There should be mention of the Royalist hopes before battle. Reference should be made to the hopes inspired by Rupert's reputation and leadership and some idea of where the battle will take place.
   - After the battle, there should be mention of the surprise attack by Parliamentarians, the failure of Rupert's cavalry and the last stand of the Whitecoats.

- There should be mention of the Parliamentarian hopes before battle, including Cromwell's disciplined cavalry and the fact that the Royalists were outnumbered.
- After the battle, there should be mention of the surprise attack, the gallantry of Fairfax, the steadiness of Cromwell's cavalry and, perhaps, the final defeat of the Whitecoats.
- A Parliamentarian might well take note of Rupert's humiliation.
- In both accounts some mention should be made of weapons and tactics.
  (15 marks)

4. (a) This question can be used here as revision. The main points to be included in the answer are as follows:
   - *Charles believed in the Divine Right of Kings and was reluctant to come to terms with Parliament.*
   - *Charles raised taxes without the consent of Parliament.*
   - *Laud made changes to the Church of England, which concerned many MPs because they thought this was a return to Catholicism.*
   - *In 1641 there was a rebellion in Ireland. Charles had to request Parliament for the money to raise an army to put down the rebellion. However, Parliament would only grant the money on the condition that they could appoint the commander.*
   - *Charles tried to arrest five MPs whilst in the House of Commons.*
   - *Parliament passed the Nineteen Propositions.* (20 marks)

   (b) The answer should include the following points:
   - *The King's rich supporters ran out of money. After his defeat at Naseby he could not afford to raise another army.*
   - *It was difficult for Charles to get men and supplies from abroad as the navy supported Parliament.*
   - *Prince Rupert was inexperienced with regard to sieges and infantry tactics.*
   - *Parliament controlled the richest part of the country, the south-east.*
   - *Parliament had a better-trained army and chose better commanders.*
   - *Parliament controlled the capital as Charles left London at the start of the war.*
   - *The Royalists made a serious error by not taking London after the Battle of Edgehill.* (10 marks)

                                                          Total for exercise: 65 marks

Exercise 7.2

1.

Charges against Charles I	Evidence for guilt	Evidence for innocence
Ruled as a tyrant	Forced loans; imprisonment without trial; ship money; attempted arrest of the five MPs, January 1642	The Puritan MPs opposed Charles because of suspicion of his Catholic wife
Made war on his own subjects	Raising the standard at Nottingham, August 1642; all events after	The Parliamentarians and their supporters were viewed as 'rebels'
Asked for help from the French and the Dutch	Private papers retrieved after the Battle of Naseby	Parliament had themselves asked for help from the Scots
Restarted the war after surrendering	Began secret negotiations with the Scots while imprisoned	Charles had surrendered to the Scots, not to Parliament

(10 marks)

(a) There is considerable historical debate here, so good answers cannot be predicted. What is certain is that the army were determined to bring the King to trial after he started the second Civil War. He was called 'Charles Stuart that man of blood' by the army because it believed that Charles should have accepted defeat and not plunged the country into another war. Before the second Civil War he negotiated with the army, Parliament and the Scots, trying to play one off against another, and his negotiations lacked sincerity. Charles's supporters would stress that the army did not represent public opinion and that Charles was legally entitled as King to do what he liked. He saw himself as protecting not only his rights but those of his subjects against a Puritan/army tyranny.

The evidence for Charles might include:
- There was no legal basis for the trial of a monarch under English law, as all law in theory came from the king.
- The trial itself was in front of a court that was not representative of the nation

as a whole, but had been gathered by the army who were determined to execute Charles.

The evidence against Charles might include:
- He had declared war by raising his standard in 1642.
- He had plotted to get assistance from France and Ireland, in other words, he hoped to use foreign troops against his own subjects.
- He also secretly negotiated with the Scots and started a second Civil War after losing the first. (20 marks)

(b) The answer should contain the following points:
- He took the legally sound line that, as King, no authority on earth could judge him.
- As a Divine Right monarch he was appointed by God and answerable to God alone.
- All the laws of England came from the monarch, so no law could try and condemn him. (10 marks)

2. A good answer should contain supporting evidence from the source. The following points should be included:
- The crowd's reaction was one of sympathy for Charles: 'huge groan' of horror.
- The complication was that the army was needed to control the crowd.
- The impression of the eye-witness is that he disapproved of the King's execution. (10 marks)

3. This is an exercise in using historical imagination and should be seen in that context. The account should, however, contain the following points:
- A clear indication of the King's bravery.
- A note of the cold weather.
- The role of the army in crowd control.
- The 'groan from the crowd as I never heard before'.
- The dipping of handkerchiefs in Charles's blood.
- Probably the smell of a huge, unwashed crowd. (10 marks)

Total for exercise: 60 marks

Exercise 7.3

1. The Rump Parliament did not provide the radical reforms that Cromwell and the army had hoped for. It did do some good, i.e. it introduced some degree of religious toleration and required all court proceedings to be conducted in English, but this was not enough for Cromwell. (5 marks)

2. The Barebones Parliament found it impossible to work together and could not agree amongst themselves on the issues. The majority were frightened of anarchy so wished for clear authority vested in a ruler. The concept of a sole ruler was one that they were familiar with. But see below (5 marks).

Additional information

A new constitution had already been drawn up called the Instrument of Government. It was the first written constitution England ever had. It gave Cromwell some limited powers, but laid down that Parliament should be called regularly and could not be dismissed for five months once it sat. More people were allowed to vote in elections and constituencies were reformed so they represented more accurately the population of the country. Cromwell was given a fixed income as commander of the armed forces, but was not an absolute ruler. The MPs of the Barebones Parliament almost certainly knew that this constitution had been drawn up when they surrendered their powers to Cromwell in December 1653.

Total for exercise: 10 marks

Exercise 7.4

1. Paulucci suggests that Cromwell has become a king in all but name. (2 marks)

2. Source B shows that Cromwell was prepared to dress and act like a monarch. (3 marks)

3. The cartoon shows Cromwell with the crown, orb and sceptre, a regal cloak, and a warrior's armour: the traditional outfit of a monarch. It shows that Cromwell had changed from initially having radical ideas, to becoming much like the king he wanted to replace. (7 marks)

4. The answer should include the following points:
    *   Cromwell had started out in the 1640s as an opponent of the monarchy.
    *   He had been the driving force behind Charles's execution.
    *   He had hoped that the republican Rump Parliament would provide good government, but was disappointed.

- He gradually became more conservative and, after accepting the Protectorship in 1653, he eventually became a king in all but name.
- The sources show him as being seen as a king and he had a ceremony in 1657 that was like a coronation.
- He fell out with Parliament and increasingly relied on the army.
- The Protectorate became like a monarchy in another way, it was hereditary.
  (8 marks)

Total for exercise: 20 marks

Exercise 7.5

1. (a) Everyday life had changed for people during the Protectorate:
    - Many of the traditional pastimes of ordinary people were frowned on or banned.
    - For example, singing, maypole dancing, drinking, cock fighting, horse racing and bear baiting were banned.
    - Christmas was also banned.
    - Sunday was to be spent on church attendance and Bible reading.
    - Theatres and inns were closed down.
    - People were expected to wear dark drab clothes rather than anything colourful.
    - Stricter and stricter codes of behaviour were expected, which led to a climate of fear. (20 marks)

    (b) Puritans banned Christmas and other pastimes for the following reasons:
    - Strict Puritans regarded Christmas as a celebration left over from Catholic times – Christ Mass.
    - It was seen as an excuse for drinking and gluttony.
    - All entertainments were seen as ungodly; they took people's minds off what they should have been thinking about: Bible reading and worship of God.
      (10 marks)

Total for exercise: 30 marks

Exercise 7.6

1. The writer has a high opinion of Cromwell: 'the merits of that most excellent Prince'.
    (2 marks)

2. Source A and Source B are useful to show how some people admired Cromwell. They should be treated with caution though. Source A is from a government newspaper of the

time while the writer of Source B, Milton, was Cromwell's Latin secretary and wrote several defences of him. To give a balanced view, sources that are neutral or hostile to Cromwell would be needed. (3 marks)

3. Many people thought that Cromwell had protected Parliament – the people's elected representatives – against the 'tyranny' of Charles I. He therefore represented the power and independence of a Parliament that was separate from the Crown. After Cromwell no monarch would think that he or she could get rid of Parliament. (7 marks)

4. If only the sources are used then the answer would be that Cromwell did deserve the praise he received after his death. If pupils use additional information from the chapter (pages 120–138) and some of their own knowledge, then a much more balanced assessment could be expected. Some of the points to be included are:
   - He prevented anarchy.
   - He secured religious toleration.
   - He defeated both the Scots and the Irish.
   - He defeated Charles II at the Battle of Worcester
   - He prevented another civil war.
   - Many people regarded him as a tyrant, especially the Irish.
   - He was never able to come to a proper agreement with his Parliaments.
   - Puritanism under Cromwell was unpopular because it interfered with people's lives and pastimes. (8 marks)

Total for exercise: 20 marks

Exercise 7.7

1. (a) The answer should include the following points:
   - Cromwell was the Commander of the army after Charles's execution.
   - He defeated both the Scots and the Irish.
   - He defeated Charles II at the battle of Worcester.
   - He removed the Rump Parliament in April 1653.
   - He became Lord Protector in December 1653.
   - He set up rule by Major-Generals in 1655.
   - He quarrelled with Parliament.
   - The Protectorate became hereditary in 1657.
   - He died in September 1658. (20 marks)

   (b) This is a question which is still a matter of historical debate and controversy. A good answer will provide balance with such points as:

- *For:*
  - *– He prevented anarchy.*
  - *– He secured a form of religious toleration.*
  - *– He prevented another civil war by defeating Charles II at Worcester.*
- *Against:*
  - *– Many people regarded him as a tyrant, especially the Irish.*
  - *– Puritanism under Cromwell was unpopular because it interfered with people's lives and pastimes.*
  - *– He was never able to come to a proper agreement with his Parliaments.*

N.B. These are only examples of possible points. The question is a good open one that may elucidate interesting responses. (10 marks)

2. (a) The following points should be included in the answer:
- *Monck was the key figure in the Restoration.*
- *He commanded a large and loyal army in Scotland.*
- *In the autumn of 1659, as England seemed to dissolve into anarchy, he marched south towards London.*
- *The Long Parliament was recalled that December.*
- *In March 1660 Monck negotiated with Charles II's advisers and the result was the Declaration of Breda.*
- *This paved the way for the Restoration.* (20 marks)

(b) *The reasons why England restored the monarchy were:*
- *Increasing squabbles between Parliament and the army meant that the country seemed to be heading for anarchy.*
- *There was a fear that this could lead to another civil war.*
- *Monck took control with his army and decided that the public wanted unity around a single figure – the King.*
- *The Declaration of Breda was very clever: it reassured people that if they had fought against Charles I, they would not be punished by Charles II; the army would be paid; Charles would not rule as a Divine Right monarch. This satisfied nearly everyone.* (10 marks)

3. This speech should contain references to the Declaration of Breda and, in particular, to the extract on page 139. The impression should be left that Charles is going to rule by consent, 'a free Parliament', and that all the division and hatreds of the last twenty years will be put aside under his rule. (10 marks)

Total for exercise: 70 marks

Chapter 8 Charles II and James II

Exercise 8.1

1. (a) *The Restoration in 1660 was the restoring of the monarchy after Cromwell's death and the collapse of the republic. Charles returned from exile with popular approval.* (3 marks)

   (b) *Dissenters were those stronger Puritans who could not accept the Anglican Church of England. They were also known as 'non-conformists'.* (3 marks)

   (c) *Regicides were those who signed the death warrant of Charles I in January 1649. There were 59 signatories of whom 39 were still alive in 1660. The term was used also to describe those who had taken part in the execution whilst not having signed the death warrant. They were punished or imprisoned.* (4 marks)

   N.B. Regicides such as Major General Harrison suffered an appalling death of hanging, drawing and quartering, a far slower and more excruciating death than Charles suffered.

2. The article might include the following:
   - The role of General Monck.
   - The Declaration of Breda.
   - The general thanksgiving and welcome for Charles II.
   - The questions that remained such as dissenters and regicides. (10 marks)

3. The following points should be included in the answer:
   - *Charles II's lifestyle was quite contrary to the Puritan lifestyle – mistresses and a carefree court.*
   - *Theatres, music, dancing and feasts returned, all of which Puritans disapproved of.*
   - *The exhumation of Cromwell's body and the punishment of the regicides would have been disapproved of by those Puritans who were also republicans.*
   - *According to the Bishop of Salisbury, 'he seemed to have no sense of religion'.* (10 marks)

Total for exercise: 30 marks

Exercise 8.2

1. (a) The following points should be included in the answer:
   - The plague started in Western Europe.
   - The plague broke out in London in 1665.
   - The plague spread rapidly due to the hot summer.
   - The King and nobility fled.
   - The death toll was officially given as 68,576 but the true number is perhaps nearer 100,000.
   - The plague was spread by rat fleas. (20 marks)

   (b) The plague was so devastating because:
   - It spread very rapidly.
   - The numbers involved were unprecedented, for example as Pepys says, there was 'sadder and sadder news of its increase'.
   - There was a huge effect on business and trade, as noted by Pepys: 'no boats on the river'. (10 marks)

2. (a) The instructions given by the Lord Mayor were as follows:
   - Infected houses had to be marked with a red cross on which the words 'Lord have mercy upon us' had to be inscribed.
   - No person could leave an infected house for at least a month after it was found to be infected. Watchmen were appointed to guard infected houses – one for the day and one for the night.
   - Women searchers were appointed to patrol the streets, monitor the deaths and report the causes of death. These searchers were not allowed to keep a shop or work as a laundress.
   - The dead were to be buried after sunset and before sunrise.
   - No pigs, dogs, cats or rabbits were to be kept in the city. (20 marks)

   (b) The following instructions would have stopped the plague from spreading:
   - Infected houses were marked and inhabitants were kept inside the house so that they did not come into contact with other people.
   - Women searchers were not allowed to keep a shop or work as laundresses; this was so that they could not sell goods that had been owned by plague victims, or wash their clothes and catch the disease.
   - The burial of the dead was at times when fewer people were around, so again this would minimise contact.

The following instructions would have been no use in preventing the spread of the plague:

- Keeping cats and dogs was banned and they were killed. This was a mistake as cats and dogs killed the rats that spread the plague. (10 marks)

3. The account should give some examples from Pepys's diary. Mention should be made of the Lord Mayor's instructions and the Bills of Mortality. The rapidity of the spread of the plague in the summer time and its dying down in winter should be in the account. (10 marks)

Total for exercise: 70 marks

Exercise 8.3

1. The plague had a terrible effect on public morale; people were terrified and depressed. It killed 70,000 (although some estimate that it was nearer 100,000). The Port of London ceased trading for six months. The Great Fire was probably less damaging. (2 marks)

2. By September 1665 the quarantine measures that had been in place were abandoned, as the authorities could no longer cope. The dead were buried in mass graves called 'plague pits'. (3 marks)

3. There is agreement on the effect on public morale: Source A describes it as 'disastrous'; Source B describes the 'helpless municipal authorities'; and Source C says that 'people were very worried'. Source B and Source C both state that the plague started in the St Giles parish. (7 marks)

4. Source B is the most useful in supporting that very little could have been done to prevent the plague because of references to 8,000 deaths per week. This implies that the authorities could not keep up their anti-plague measures because they were simply overwhelmed by the scale of the plague. (8 marks)

Total for exercise: 20 marks

Exercise 8.4

1. (a) The Great Fire began in Pudding Lane at the bakers shop owned by Thomas Farynor who did not check his ovens before going to bed. (2 marks)

   (b) There was no fire brigade. It then reached the riverside wharves full of very flammable materials. The houses were close together and the decision to create firebreaks was taken too late. (3 marks)

2. (a) A historian can learn the following from Pepys's diary:
   - Pepys's account is vivid.
   - He was there at the time.
   - He was an intelligent, well-informed 'civil servant'.
   - He shows how quickly the fire spread: 'at three in the morning' it seemed to have started; later he writes of three hundred homes burned down.
   - He gives an account of the evacuation of the city and people trying to save their valuables.
   - He gives a picture of the destroyed city: '... all the town burned, and a miserable sight of St Paul's ...' (20 marks)

   (b) The only reason to treat Pepys's account with caution is that to get a full picture we would need more eye-witness accounts, especially of the beginning of the fire which Pepys only saw from a distance. (10 marks)

   N.B. Pepys is a good and accurate witness, so there must be a degree of opinion allowed in this answer, which could 'question the question'.

3. This might follow the outline of Pepys's experience, but also mention the cause of the fire and the blowing up of houses to create firebreaks. (10 marks)

Total for exercise: 45 marks

Exercise 8.5

1. (a) The Clarendon Code contained the Corporation Act, where all municipal officials had to take Anglican Communion; the Act of Uniformity, which made the Book of Common Prayer compulsory; the Coventicle Act, which forbade meetings for unauthorised worship; and the Five Mile Act, which forbade non-conformist ministers from coming within five miles of incorporated towns or the place of their former livings. It was used to uphold the supremacy of the Anglican Church and control any dissenters. (4 marks)

   (b) Charles wished to grant toleration to Roman Catholics and dissenters and so issued the Declaration of Indulgence so that they could worship freely. Parliament was largely composed of Anglican Protestants and disapproved. (3 marks)

   (c) The Test Act required all office holders to swear that they were Protestants. It was aimed against Catholics. (3 marks)

2. (a) The answer should contain the following points:
   - Charles wished to allow Roman Catholics and dissenters to worship freely.
   - He issued the Declaration of Indulgence.

- However, the majority of MPs were strict Protestants and so they passed the Test Act, requiring all government officials to swear an oath that they were Protestants.
- This led to religious tension – there was an underlying fear of Catholics.
- Titus Oates exploited this general fear by claiming that there was a plot to put Charles's Catholic brother on the throne – the Popish Plot.
- A bill was proposed, the Exclusion Bill, to exclude James from the throne.
- This led to anti-Catholic riots and many Catholics being tried for treason, executed or imprisoned.
- However, Oates had made the story up.
- Although the unrest settled down, many people were still fearful of Catholics and the anti-Catholic feelings remained.
- This fear again led to a plot to assassinate Charles and James – the Rye House Plot. (20 marks)

(b) The answer should cover the following points:
- The Popish Plot provoked a lot of anti-Catholic feeling.
- An attempt was made to pass the Exclusion Bill to remove Charles's Catholic brother James from the line of succession.
- In the event the Plot was disproved, and the Exclusion Bill was blocked.
- The Rye House Plot helped Charles by provoking public sympathy for him and his brother James.
- The brothers were popular once more, the Whigs were discredited.
- James was able to accede to the throne with much less opposition in 1685. (10 marks)

Total for exercise: 40 marks

Exercise 8.6

The answer should include the following points:
- The extracts actually deal with rather different aspects of Charles's character and actions.
- The area of agreement might be the charm of Charles: 'a softness of temper that charmed all'; 'good liking of his people'.
- The Bishop of Salisbury writes of his unreliability, whereas Pepys writes of 'no money, no reputation' and laziness. He even writes that people began to look back to Cromwell's rule with some approval. The Bishop does not mention this aspect, which deals with foreign policy.

- *Therefore, the sources complement each other, rather than actually supporting each other, and build up an unflattering portrait of Charles.* (20 marks)

Total for exercise: 20 marks

Exercise 8.7

1. Source A makes the following points about the reasons behind the Glorious Revolution:
   - *James abused his powers: he suspended Parliament, collected taxes unlawfully, and undermined the independence of both the law and the universities.*
   - *He also tried to impose Catholicism on a Protestant country and the country objected.* (2 marks)

2. Source B implies that although John Churchill was loyal at first to James II, that loyalty had limits. He was partly influenced by religion: as an Anglican he was worried about James's Catholic beliefs. But he was an opportunist; when it seemed that William was bound to succeed he changed sides. (3 marks)

3. Source A and Source C agree on the following:
   - *James abused his power.*
   - *He tried to rule without reference to the law and Parliament.*
   - *He wished to restrict religious liberty and bring in Roman Catholicism.* (7 marks)

4. This is a difficult question; 'inevitable' is not a word that historians are fond of. In support of the view the following might be argued:
   - *James lost the loyalty and support of the majority of the country.*
   - *He fled partly because he thought that he might share his father's fate.*
   - *James's policies could only lead to revolution or civil war. An attempt to restore Catholicism and rule as a Divine Right monarch was doomed from the start.* (8 marks)

Total for exercise: 20 marks

Exercise 8.8

1. Advice that could have been given to James II in 1685 might take one of two lines:
   - As king you have the power to change the position of Roman Catholics and to restore the strength of the Crown. N.B. This line of advice was that given to James by his absolutist advisers and proved disastrous.
   - The second line of advice would be a conciliatory one:
     – Work with Parliament.

- Accept that the English people will not allow the country to become Roman Catholic.
- Respect the laws and customs of the country. (10 marks)

2. (a) The answer should include the following points:
- In 1685 when James became King, there was less hostility towards him than previously felt.
- He had reasonable relations with parliament.
- However, following the Monmouth Rebellion and Bloody Assizes his relations with Parliament deteriorated and he dissolved Parliament.
- There was still an underlying fear of Catholicism and many thought that he wanted to restore England to the Catholic religion.
- In 1687 James lost a court case when seven bishops refused to accept his religious changes, the first time in history that this had happened.
- Thus, except for Roman Catholics, there was little support for James.
- This was because he had, in most peoples' views, undermined the constitution and wished to set up a Roman Catholic monarchy. (20 marks)

(b) The answer should include the following points:
- By 1688, most people had come to the conclusion that James was trying to set up a Roman Catholic monarchy and that he was a threat to the law, the constitution and English liberties.
- Already there was an alternative to James, William of Orange, who had a claim to the throne, as did his wife, and who was a Protestant.
- His attempt to force the bishops to read the Declaration of Indulgence only confirmed the view that he would do whatever he wanted.
- The Bloody Assizes of 1685 had left the impression that James was a vindictive ruthless monarch.
- The birth of the Prince of Wales in June 1688 meant that James had an heir to carry on his policies.
- In these circumstances William of Orange's invasion of November 1688 was welcomed. (10 marks)

Total for exercise: 40 marks

Exercise 8.9

This exercise is based on the pupils' own researches and choices. The guiding principles should be:

- Any research should be evaluated as to provenance and reliability, for example using the internet has to be associated with knowing who wrote the material.
- Credit should be given for the ability to assess the significance of various artistic productions and scientific advances.
- Good answers will be based on proper research and show originality and balance. It is not possible to provide model answers to these questions, the pupil response will vary but the above guidelines may be helpful.

1. 10 marks

2. (a) 20 marks
    (b) 10 marks

3. (a) 20 marks
    (b) 10 marks

4. (a) 20 marks
    (b) 10 marks

5. (a) 20 marks
    (b) 10 marks

Total for exercise: 130 marks

Chapter 9 William and Mary, and Anne

Exercise 9.1

1. *What the Crown gained in the first few years of William and Mary's reign:*
   - *Security with the defeat of James II.*
   - *Regular grant of money, known as the Civil List.*

   What Parliament gained in the first few years of William and Mary's reign:
   - *The Triennial Act, allowing Parliament to be called at least every three years.*
   - *Succession to be determined by Parliament.*
   - *There was to be no taxation except by Parliamentary consent.*
   - *There was to be no standing army in peacetime.*
   - *Freedom of speech for MPs.* (10 marks)

2. *Parliament was the more powerful by the end of William's reign for the following reasons:*
   - *The Triennial Act, which allowed Parliament to be called at least once every three years.*
   - *There was Parliamentary control of taxation and Royal accounts were to be scrutinised by Parliament.*
   - *Parliament now decided the succession to the throne.*
   - *There was no royal standing army in peacetime.* (10 marks)

3. (a) *The events of the Glorious Revolution were as follows:*
   - *Following James's court defeat, the Whigs and Tories invited William to come to England to save Protestantism in England and to protect the rights of his wife.*
   - *James's second wife gave birth to the Prince of Wales; however, it was rumoured that the baby had been smuggled in (he was 'the warming pan baby').*
   - *William invaded and subsequently James fled to France.*
   - *Importantly, there was no civil war – it was a bloodless revolution, at least in England.*
   - *William and Mary became joint monarchs.*
   - *However they had to sign the Bill of Rights.*
   - *They also had to agree to the Triennial Act, which allowed Parliament to be called at least once every three years.*
   - *There was Parliamentary control of taxation and Royal accounts were to be scrutinised by Parliament.*
   - *Parliament now decided the succession to the throne.*
   - *There was no royal standing army in peacetime.* (20 marks)

(b) *These events were given the name the 'Glorious Revolution' because:*
- *There was no civil war.*
- *William and Mary's accession was bloodless.*
- *The events prevented an absolutist Catholic monarchy.*
- *They preserved English liberties.* (**10 marks**)

Total for exercise: 50 marks

Exercise 9.2

1. (a) The following points should be included in the answer:
    - *Following the end of the Glorious Revolution, it was now Parliament's responsibility to decide the succession to the throne.*
    - *As William and Mary had no children, Parliament needed to make a decision.*
    - *Mary's half-brother was Catholic so Parliament decided, with the Act of Succession, that the throne should pass to Mary's younger sister, Anne.*
    - *The Act barred the descendants of James II and Mary of Modena from inheriting the Crown.*
    - *After Anne's death (she had no surviving children), the succession was to pass to James I's granddaughter Sophia of Hanover.*
    - *This led to the House of Hanover succeeding to the throne.* (**20 marks**)

   (b) The following points should be included:
    - *The next king of Scotland was to be James Edward Stuart, Mary's half-brother and a Catholic.*
    - *Scotland did not support the war on France in 1702.*
    - *There was a danger of a Franco-Scottish alliance.* (**10 marks**)

2. (a) The following points should be included in the answer:
    - *Some MPs thought it would be useful to unite the English and Scottish Parliaments as relations were deteriorating.*
    - *Although the Scots were less keen, they were brought round by being granted money to be paid to Scottish merchants who had lost money in English companies trading abroad.*
    - *The Act of Union was passed, uniting the two Parliaments.*
    - *Forty-six Scottish MPs would sit in the Commons.*
    - *Sixteen peers would sit in the House of Lords.*
    - *The Scottish Parliament would cease to exist.*
    - *Scotland would keep its own established church.*
    - *Coinage, taxation, army, trade, law and Parliament would be shared with England.* (**20 marks**)

(b) The Act of Union was beneficial to both England and Scotland in the following ways:
- Scotland gained access to English markets and trade.
- This brought prosperity to Scotland, at least to the Lowlands.
- England gained security; there was now no danger of a Franco-Scottish alliance leading to invasion from Scotland. (10 marks)

Total for exercise: 60 marks

Exercise 9.3

Questions 1, 2 and 4 rely on personal research. Answers should give clear details, including dates, movements of troops and tactics.

1. 10 marks

2. (a) 20 marks
    (b) 10 marks

3. The picture gives the impression of:
- Marlborough as an inspiring leader.
- A degree of confusion, as in any 18th century battle.
- It is of limited value as details are hard to discern.
- Also, it was painted well after the event and we do not know if the painter had actual knowledge of the battle. (10 marks)

4. 10 marks

Total for exercise: 60 marks

Chapter 10 George I and II

Exercise 10.1

1. King George was disliked for the following reasons:
   - He disliked the English.
   - He spoke little English.
   - He had an awkward manner.
   - Some opposed the Hanoverian succession. (5 marks)

2. (a) The main causes and events of the Jacobite rebellion were as follows:
   - There were some who opposed the Hanoverian succession and wished the Stuart dynasty to take back the throne.
   - These people were called Jacobites.
   - In 1715 the Earl of Mar proclaimed the 'old pretender' James Edward Stuart king.
   - He raised a force of 10,000–12,000 men.
   - At the same time there were risings in Wales and the south-west.
   - On 13th November a Jacobite force was defeated at the Battle of Preston.
   - Mar met government forces at the Battle of Sheriffmuir.
   - Mar was unable to break out of the Scottish Highlands and head south.
   - James Edward Stuart returned to France in 1716 as the rebellion collapsed. (20 marks)

   (b) The following points should be made regarding the Hanoverian succession:
   - The failure of the 1715 rebellion meant that many who were inclined to be Jacobites began to believe that their cause was hopeless.
   - These people therefore accepted the Hanoverian succession.
   - The army garrisons in Scotland, and the formation of the Black Watch, kept rebels under control. (10 marks)

   Total for exercise: 35 marks

Exercise 10.2

1. (a) Parliament was composed of Whigs and Tories; most MPs were county gentlemen. Whigs supported the Hanoverian dynasty and were associated with business and commerce. Tories tended to be more inclined to be sympathetic to the Stuarts, and disliked the London money men and traders. (3 marks)

(b) *The Cabinet had its origins in the council that looked after affairs whilst George was in Hanover. The Cabinet was the name given to the room where the council met.* (2 marks)

(c) *The Septennial Act set out that a new Parliament had to be called every seven years, as opposed to every three years.* (2 marks)

(d) *The South Sea Bubble was caused by the South Sea Company, which had taken on responsibility for the National Debt, issuing too many shares that plunged in value. This led to a crash in the financial markets.* (3 marks)

2. (a) The answer should contain the following points:
   - *By the end of the reign of George I, Britain owned territory in America and the West Indies.*
   - *These American colonies had been started by a range of different people, including the Puritans who had left England and adventurers seeking their fortune.*
   - *Traders in America and the West Indies began to buy slaves from Africa to work on the plantations.*
   - *This led to the Triangular Trade.*
   - *In the Triangular Trade, British traders exported alcohol, guns, horses and pottery to Africa. These goods were exchanged for slaves.*
   - *The slaves were then taken to the West Indies and America to work on the plantations.*
   - *The produce from the plantations, such as sugar, tobacco and coffee, was then brought to England via the ports of Bristol and Liverpool.* (20 marks)

   (b) *British traders made three profits from the triangular trade:*
   - *The profit on exports to Africa.*
   - *The selling of slaves.*
   - *The import and re-export of sugar, tobacco, cotton and coffee.* (10 marks)

3. (a) The answer should contain the following points:
   - *When the King was absent, a leading Cabinet minister chaired the Cabinet meetings and reported to the King.*
   - *Robert Walpole was the leading Cabinet minister from 1721 to 1743.*
   - *Walpole rose to power as the man who could resolve the crisis caused by the South Sea Bubble.*
   - *He managed to create a system whereby nearly all government appointments were in his hands. No one else had ever had this control of patronage.*

- *He controlled most of the important parts of government.*
- *He destroyed his political opponents, the Tories, by suggesting they were all Jacobites. (20 marks)*

(b) *He became known as Britain's first Prime Minister for the following reasons:*
- *No previous minister of the Crown had succeeded in becoming so indispensable.*
- *He had control over both foreign and domestic policy and all decisions went through him. (10 marks)*

4. This answer will depend on the quality of research, detail and persuasiveness of the prospectus. (10 marks)

Total for exercise: 80 marks

Exercise 10.3

1. (a) *The 1745 Rebellion failed for the following reasons:*
   - *Charles Edward Stuart was an incompetent leader:*
     - *He retreated from Derby.*
     - *He decided to fight at Culloden Moor.*
     - *He failed to listen to Lord George Murray's advice.*
     - *He was forced to retreat at Culloden Moor.*
   - *He did not have enough support from France.*
   - *The Highlanders who had joined him became tired and hungry.*
   - *He lacked any effective artillery.*
   - *There was sustained fire by Cumberland's troops at Culloden.*
   - *The Highlanders were reluctant to advance into England. (20 marks)*

   (b) *The most important reason for the failure was probably the Highlanders' lack of modern equipment, modern fighting techniques and a proper supply chain. These things could have secured a victory despite weak leadership. (10 marks)*

2. The advice should contain the following points:
   - To wait for more French support.
   - To ensure good supplies.
   - To listen to his most intelligent and experienced adviser, Lord George Murray. (10 marks)

3. This answer should show how the English, on one hand, and Scottish sympathisers of Bonnie Prince Charlie, on the other, would have had different

views about the battle. A Scottish version would emphasise the bravery of the Highlanders and the cruelty of Cumberland; the English version would emphasise the steadiness of the Redcoats and the 'primitive' nature of the Highlanders. There are of course many different responses to this question, so a clear understanding of the events and use of evidence is paramount. (20 marks)

Total for exercise: 60 marks

Exercise 10.4

1. *From Source A it would seem that Bonnie Prince Charlie's chances of success were very slim. Charles should have waited for a better opportunity.* (2 marks)

2. *The government's victory was the result of a mixture of volley firing and the use of the bayonet. The Scots were outgunned and even reduced to throwing stones.* (3 marks)

3. *Source B shows Barrell's regiment in close quarter fighting with the Scots. It agrees with Source C in that 'Barrell's regiment beat them with their bayonets', which is shown in Source B.* (7 marks)

4. To a degree, any reasoned response to this question, which uses evidence and material from pages 178–184, must be accepted, but it can be argued that Source D is the least helpful and Source C the most in that it shows that at Culloden it was disciplined fire power that won the day.

    Source A has some use as background information: if Bonnie Prince Charlie had had French troops then the result might have been different; whilst Source B supports Source C. (8 marks)

Total for exercise: 20 marks

Appendix

Essay questions: generic mark scheme

Selective description

e.g. Describe the key features of… etc.

Mark	Target	Causation / recall of knowledge
1–8	Level 1	Simple statements offering some features / ideas supported by some knowledge; embryonic, inaccurate or irrelevant knowledge; lacking real coherence and structure.
9–15	Level 2	More developed statements giving features supported by more relevant knowledge; thinly substantiated passages; uncertain overall structure.
16–20	Level 3	Developed selection of features with sound substantiation and structure; good range of features; for top of level, answer will show clear linkage and relevant importance of features.

Evaluation / Analysis

e.g. Explain why…

Mark	Target	Evaluation of factors against one another / definitions of success and failure / contextual assessment
1–4	Level 1	Simple statement offering basic and largely unfocused opinion.
5–8	Level 2	More developed analysis with some coherent judgement; some substantiation of assertions.
9–10	Level 3	Precisely selected knowledge in a clear framework of argument; strong and developed analysis / assessment with cogent judgements; strong substantiation of assertions.

Evidence questions: mark scheme. Total: 25 marks

Mark	Target	Comprehension of source
1	Level 1	Incomplete or imprecise answer.
2	Level 2	Answer which more clearly substantiates from the source.

Mark	Target	Comprehension of source
1	Level 1	Incomplete or imprecise answer.
2–3	Level 2	More developed understanding.

Mark	Target	**Corroboration by cross-referencing sources**
1	**Level 1**	Simple statement which makes a basic comment on a source.
2–4	**Level 2**	Answer which is more developed, connecting Source C to another source with a substantiated argument.
5–6	**Level 3**	Fully-developed answer which examines all three sources using a substantiated argument.

Mark	Target	**Evaluation of sources for utility / consideration of provenance**
1–2	**Level 1**	Simple statement which makes a basic comment on a source, looking only at the content.
3–5	**Level 2**	Answer which recognises that different sources can be useful for different purposes. For lower reaches of this band, relies on generalised comments, such as 'it depends on what you want to know' or 'all sources are useful in one way or another'.
6	**Level 3**	Developed and substantiated analysis of all three sources, looking at both content and provenance, and contextual appreciation that they all, in their own way, help our understanding of the argument.

Mark	Target	**Making a judgement about an interpretation, relating analysis of sources to contextual knowledge**
1–3	**Level 1**	Answer which makes little or no use of sources or makes little or no use of own knowledge. There is poor argument, little or no substantiation and only vague / embryonic statement of agreement / disagreement.
4–6	**Level 2**	More developed answer, making better use of sources in terms of content and with some own knowledge. *Or* good use of own knowledge but weaker use of sources.
7–8	**Level 3**	Answer which makes full and intelligent use of all three sources, examining content and interleaving answer with accurate and pertinent own knowledge. For top of this level, the candidate will have written a very cogent and well-structured answer, with judicious appreciation of the sources and own knowledge in equal measure.

ISEB
**Independent Schools
Examinations Board**

Galore Park
PRACTICE EXERCISES

GALORE PARK

Why Practice Exercises?

- Perfect for 11+, 13+ and scholarship entrance exam preparation

- Packed full of lots of practice exercises so that pupils are fully prepared for their exam

- Enables pupils to identify gaps in knowledge so that they can focus their revision

- Helps to familiarise pupils with the format of the exam so that they don't get any nasty surprises in the exam room!

- Answers also available so that pupils can check whether they have answered correctly or need to do further revision

To receive **10% discount** on **History Practice Exercises 13+**,
please enter code GPAD07 in the Discount Code field
when you place your order at

www.galorepark.co.uk

IPG Education Publisher of the Year 2009

ISEB
Independent Schools
Examinations Board

Galore Park
STUDY SKILLS

GALORE PARK

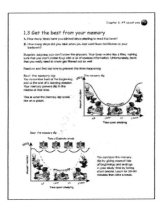

Why Study Skills?

- Perfect for any pupil aged 8–13

- Packed full of lots of practical advice about how to revise and how to be a smarter learner

- Enables pupils to identify their learning style so that they can revise using the techniques that work for them

- Includes plenty of examples of revision techniques such as mind maps and memory games which will help pupils to retain information more easily

- Workbook format enables pupils to keep a learning log which they can keep referring back to

To receive **10% discount** on **Study Skills,** please enter
code GPAD07 in the Discount Code field
when you place your order at

www.galorepark.co.uk

IPG Education Publisher of the Year 2009

ISEB
Independent Schools
Examinations Board

Galore Park
ISEB REVISION GUIDES

GALORE PARK

Why ISEB Revision Guides?

- Perfect for 11+, 13+ and scholarship entrance exam preparation

- Consolidates the key information for the subject area into ONE resource making revision a breeze!

- Enables pupils to identify gaps in knowledge so that they can focus their revision

- Worked examples help pupils to see how they can gain the best possible marks

- Each guide includes a small amount of practice material and the answers to test understanding

- All guides are fully up to date with the latest syllabus changes to ensure pupils are revising the correct material

To receive **10% discount** on **History ISEB Revision Guide**, please enter code GPAD07 in the Discount Code field when you place your order at

www.galorepark.co.uk

IPG Education Publisher of the Year 2009